Sanskrit Drama

A Critical Reappraisal

Sanskrit Drama

A Critical Reappraisal

Madhusudan Pati

AUTHORSPRESS

Worldwide Circulation through Authorspress Global Network
First Published in 2021
by
Authorspress
Q-2A Hauz Khas Enclave, New Delhi-110 016 (India)
Phone: (0) 9818049852
E-mail: authorspressgroup@gmail.com
Website: www.authorspressbooks.com

Sanskrit Drama: A Critical Reappraisal

ISBN 978-93-90891-92-4

Printed in India at Kensington Press

Offered at the holy feet of
H.H. Swami Chidananda Saraswati Maharaj

Acknowledgement

Part of a doctoral dissertation prepared in 1979, this came out as a book in 1991. Regrettably, it contained a very large number of misprints and also a few omissions. A corrected edition that was warranted did not materialise. Recently Professor M.S. Kushwaha, retired faculty from the Lucknow University, happened to strongly reiterate his earlier suggestion for a cleaner reprint, thus triggering the present undertaking. The author thanks him for his kind interest and hopes the book – now carrying a new title – is found useful by students of Sanskrit drama.

The author gratefully recalls how two honoured departed souls – Dr. Jagannath Chakravorty, Professor of English, Jadavpur University and Dr. Bhabatosh Chatterjee, Vice Chancellor, Rabindra Bharati University – had encouraged this publication on Classical Indian drama.

The author fondly remembers the enthusiasm evinced by Dr. Chittaranjan Misra in the matter of this publication.

The author thanks the present publishing organisation, Authorspress, Delhi for their support.

Madhusudan Pati

Contents

CHAPTER 1

Introduction

The great Indian Classical plays, and the monumental dramatic treatise, *Natyashastra*, give the impression of a highly sophisticated and self-contained aesthetic world. The intellectual and cultural milieu reflected in traditional literature also supports a similar view, encouraging one to visualise a harmonious, settled, classically-controlled universe. Historical researches in the modern times have, however, revealed a different picture. For all its solid facade of established conventions and values, the Indian subcontinent was experiencing a series of upheavals at the social, political and philosophical levels[1] during the period when Sanskrit drama was attaining maturity. The Indian people did, of course, succeed in maintaining a certain steadiness through all the changing dimensions of their historical life. But they did not really allow themselves to sink into a state of servile conformism. While the bold experimentalism and innovativeness in the realms of ancient culture and politics have received some attention in the post-Independence period[2], the modalities and mores in the sphere of literary appreciation have, for the most part, remained unchanged. Literary criticism is yet to respond adequately to the controlled dynamism of life which ancient Sanskrit plays so beautifully and variously portray.

Emergence of new perspectives has been disappointingly rare, and not because of any dearth of points of critical departure. Critics of Bhasa, for instance, almost without exception, refer to certain fundamental innovations effected in his plays in the context of the tradition enunciated by Bharata. But few, if ever, pause to enquire into the nature of the dramatic compulsion behind them.[3] A certain insidious conservatism seems to have taken hold of the indigenous tradition of Sanskrit dramatic studies. And most of the Western critics on Sanskrit drama who attempted to break new ground – Macdonell and Keith, for instance – are found to be similarly hemmed in, forced by only a different set of orthodoxies. Between the traditional Sanskrit *Pundit* who merely states that in presenting death on the stage Bhasa departed from the canon, and Keith, who argues that Duryodhana being a villain Bhasa did not violate traditional injunction, there is really very little difference in terms of significant critical understanding.

Broad correctives have been offered now and then. Indu Shekhar's study of Sanskrit drama[4], designed, among other things, to emphasize the influence of popular, *'loka-dharmi'* plays, is one such work which seeks to bring about a change in critical outlook. But, again, projection of such new perspectives has not set in motion a dynamic process of critical inquiry leading to a fuller understanding of individual plays. Influence of Western dramatic criticism, similarly, which surfaces fitfully and tantalisingly in many of the Indian studies in Sanskrit drama has not effected any fundamental reorientation of critical thinking. For instance, cursory references are sometimes made to a 'Shakespearian' synthesis of high and low in some of the Sanskrit plays, but the critical possibilities inherent in the comparison are left unexplored. A handful of studies have, no doubt, appeared during the last few decades which evince an interest in certain fresh, unconventional approaches to Indian drama. Thus A.P. Singh in his study of Bhavabhuti[5] tries to take up *Uttara Ramacharitam* with the kind of critical concern that was evidenced in D.L. Roy's study[6] of the play half a century earlier. But even among relatively less conventional discussions on Sanskrit drama such as these, one rarely comes across an adequate analysis of text designed to convey some fresh understanding or to create a modern appeal. The new insights, for the most part, are confined to specific issues.

If studies in thematic and tonal patterns in Indian Classical plays have been embarrassingly few in number, the responsibility would seem to lie, primarily, with the Classical theoreticians. Their schematisations were so exhaustive, and their authority over the writers apparently so exacting and exclusive, that it was not easy for later critics to suspect that the plays could ever function otherwise, deviating from the prescriptions laid down in the manuals. The marvellous sophistication which drama and criticism achieved in the Classical times has thus been a major impediment to free critical analysis later. Most commentators on Sanskrit drama have felt enthralled and awed by the stupendous authority and scientific precision of ancient criticism and have continued to talk of standard categories like *rasa, bhava, nayaka*, etc. nursing the belief that the responsibility of critical explication could be adequately discharged with the aid of those time-honoured apparatuses. After Viswanatha, precisely during the time that ancient literary criticism in the

West was revived, revised, and a vast body of modern critical formulations were developed, Sanskrit criticism was kept chained to an older tradition and steadily allowed to drift farther and farther from the modern approaches. Consequently, a certain general consensus began to emerge that Sanskrit drama operated within a neatly delimited ambit, and the major extant plays exhibited such superb sophistication and control that precise 'Classical' affirmations in respect of them seemed not merely desirable, but inevitable.

The vast mass of criticism of Indian Classical drama, confining itself as it does to certain conventional modes is, therefore, likely to evoke a suspicion of esotericism and insularity not merely in the minds of foreigners, but also among the large majority of educated young Indians today. A rich dramatic tradition is thus in danger of being dated and atrophied. One notes in this context the marvellous resurgence of interest in Greek drama witnessed in Europe in modern times. No such creative linkage with the past distinguishes our modern theatre, except for an occasional revival or new rendering here and there. And this, in spite of the fact that Indian Classical dramatic literature offers a rich quarry of aesthetic-cultural values and technical methods to creatively explore.

As Leo Aylen[8] urges in respect of Greek drama, the spirit and modalities of Sanskrit drama, too, deserve to be revived and appreciated afresh in the interest of a sounder human culture. Such a critical resuscitation is both possible and necessary. Indian Classical drama is in a special sense universal, some of it concerned almost wholly with the permanent seats of joy and grief in the human psyche, to the exclusion of most other topical, passing verities of life. Moreover, it commits itself to a supremely satisfying pleasure-principle, and to an exultant, optimistic vision of life, without in any manner vulgarising the passions or being crudely sentimental. Since it is grounded upon an extraodinarily refined aesthetic taste it also contributes to a chastening of sensibility. Its masterful fusion of prose and poetry, of the temporal and the universal, of values of joy and duty, of worldliness and otherworldliness, could be a profound education – both moral and aesthetic – for modern man.

Application of Western critical approaches for elucidation of Indian Classical drama should, therefore, be an engaging literary adventure. Objections may, of course, be raised against such a critical procedure on the ground that what is fruitful in a given historical or literary context may prove to be inept and unsound in another. Since basic aesthetic differences between the two traditions cannot be ruled out, Indian

Classical drama and its milieu, it might be claimed, are so widely divergent from the Western dramatic traditions that transference of critical methodology from one to the other would be both inappropriate and misleading. That such differences exist is not, of course, to be debated; what is to be examined, however, is whether the differences are so basic as to preclude a meaningful critical interaction of perspectives and procedures.

Western criticism itself, for that matter, has not remained free from critical hazards of a similar kind involving confabulation of traditions. For example, drama in and after the Renaissance became predominantly character-oriented, and produced in its trail a number of critical tenets which were at variance with the Greek dramatic norms. But in spite of the inherent danger of critical confusion, juxtaposition of the two traditions has resulted in substantial critical gains in either territory. It might have, on occasions, led to certain misconceptions[9], but on the whole it has been a very productive critical enterprise. A similar critical contact between Sanskrit and European dramatic traditions is yet to be established. A certain inhibition bordering on distrust exists even among the comparatists in this regard. It may be seen how, many of the scholarly studies which are designed to offer comparative statements on Indian and Western theatres do not often venture into rigorous comparative analysis. The book by Laxmi Narayan Lal[10] may be taken as a typical illustration: he sets out to offer a study in comparison, but is content to furnish merely extended summaries of the two traditions.

In recent times Indian scholars have, no doubt, brought out some very interesting studies in comparative aesthetics. K.C. Pandey[11], Acharya Valadev Upadhyay[12], and G. B. Mohan[13], among others, highlight the exciting critical possibilities of drawing together the two major streams of aesthetics – Western and Indian. One is sorely disappointed, however, when one looks for similarly useful textual criticism. It needs to be emphasized at this point that the kind of critical effort being advocated here does not imply just an enumeration of parallels or naming the incompatibles between the Eastern and the Western dramatic postulates. Such simple, straightforward glosses have been provided in abundance by scholars in recent years. But few are willing to boldly take up the next step – formulation of a more complex, universal set of values by drawing upon the resources of both the traditions, and engaging in critical analysis of texts from a synthetic perspective. Again and again, one notices scholars – Singhal, for instance, in his book *Aristotle and Bharata*[14] – drawing back and confining themselves to the less demanding business of simple exposition and cataloguing of different points of view. In order to overcome this inhibition, it is necessary to make practical textual studies in large numbers by adopting methods and principles from either realm and demonstrating their critical use.

Introduction of Western critical approaches into the domain of Sanskrit dramatic criticism is an interesting, if difficult, experiment full of promise. A word of caution may be necessary in this context. Such a critical engagement should ensure that the essential dissimilarities between the two traditions are not glossed over or ignored. Critical exchange can offer acceptable and significant results only if the contrasted values and orientations are respected and kept in mind. We may, in passing, try to appreciate this need for caution by briefly discussing dramatic characterisation, an area where critical misreading has been frequent.

Although Western drama presents wonderfully variegated studies in character, interest in the Western theatre-except in certain modern forms – has centred relatively more on what happens to the character than on his essential being. Actions are provided in close, breathless succession, and the audience is excited more by situations and events than by a deeper feel of character. The Indian *Sahridaya* (aesthete, connoisseur), on the other hand, went to the theatre primarily to relish *rasa.* Contrastedly, if a play concentrated relatively more on character than on events as such, as does *Hamlet*, it was likely to constitute an aesthetic difficulty for the average Western theatre-goer who would find the play rather too slow and meditative for his taste. What the audience in the traditional Western theatre was treated to was an exciting *career* of a character rather than comprehensive inwardness with certain governing 'emotions' (*bhava*) in that personality. What was foregrounded was a story rather than a passion – the tragical *history* of Doctor Faustus.

Even in *Othello* where the story is of a kind that brings the play somewhat close to the Indian theatre, the Western preference is clear. It has to be emphasised that, contrary to the assumptions of Wells and Gowda[15], the play is fundamentally antithetical to the spirit of Indian drama; its concentration on the element of savage jealousy in the hero would have been unacceptable to the writer of the higher kind of Indian *nataka.* No doubt, there is a distinct similarity of dramatic interest. But even though the interest of the playwright seems to be incisively centred on a passion – that of *Karuna* – the theatre-emphasis natural to the Elizabethan stage bends it towards exciting progression of actions and events. Classical Sanskrit plays, for their part, also introduced a good deal of action, but the action was there to project the essentials of character. This can be seen even in a play most given to action, namely, *Mrichchakatikam*. Action, in respect of both Vasantasena and Charudatta, in course of the first five Acts, is minimal; the entire stretch is so contrived as to generate in the mind of the audience a progressively closer and more intense experience of character. Since the personality and passions were his primary objects, the Sanskrit dramatist did not hesitate to reduce the so-called 'dramatic' action in the interest of vivid description and enactment of passion. Act III of Bhavabhuti's *Uttara Ramacharitam* furnishes yet another telling illustration of this aesthetic choice.

The one European playwright who seeks to preserve almost an oriental centrality of character is Racine[16]. Both Racinian and Sanskrit drama confine themselves to well-chosen, select emotions. But their dramatic designs are different. Whereas Racine suddenly catapults the spectator to an intense peak, the Indian Classical playwright projects character in a more comprehensive and gradual manner, leading the audience to be immersed in empathy. Racine awes, and keeps the audience spellbound by his powerful projection of emotions. But the very extraordinariness and vehemence of passion, created so abruptly, would keep an audience somewhat uneasily distanced. Characters in Kalidasa, contrastedly, are designed to charm and enthrall an audience: while the sophisticated dramatic conventions keep the spectator aesthetically distanced, the mood of the character is gradually and intimately unravelled, allowing him to grow into the self-same mood and emotion in a very natural, spontaneous manner. This does not, however, imply a narrow selectivity of taste or outlook. Although Keith does not appreciate[17] the fact, Kalidasa is interested in the total scheme of human things, and handles character in a more inclusive manner than does Racine.

In order that purity, finish and concentration could be achieved, Racine has to sacrifice range. Moreover, the taste of his audience keeps him from dramatising tenderly gratifying emotions of the kind we relish in, say, Kalidasa's *Abhijnana Shakuntalam*. But of all Western dramatists he alone would have earned some real admiration of Indian Classical *sahridayas*, one main reason being his reluctance to use character for sundry purposes spanning social reform and philosophical formulation. The package-treatment of character and the kind of ambivalence in characterisation one encounters in most European plays would have appeared a highly exceptionable matter to the Indian dramatist. He went to character not for sheer theatrical excitement, or for socio-metaphysical illumination, but for the experience of *rasa.* The character was all-important for the purpose, and so he portrayed character in a far more chastened and restrained manner than did his Western counterpart. If, therefore, the Indian character has appeared too generalised and typical to the Western audience, the Western protagonist would have seemed only too personal and idiosyncratic to the Classical Indian.

It would be misleading if the critic does not keep in mind the basic dissimilarities of dramatic handling of character in the two traditions, and goes forward to appreciate Indian drama as if it were an off-shoot of the Elizabethan theatre. But it would, today, be equally pointless to discuss character in Indian Classical drama strictly in line with the notings in the *Natyashastra.* Certainly it is necessary that the characterisation is, first of all, understood with reference to the kind of drama, of *Karya,* and of *rasa,* within whose critical ambit a certain character is created. But once the activity of creation begins, departures from standard critical layouts, in varying extents, become inevitable, even while conforming to the basic tenets of the critical canon, the dramatic character, if successful, would always achieve a fuller, more rounded and complex personality, simply because it is now a 'living' character. And since a living dramatic character naturally comes to acquire human properties that are universal in quality, it can certainly be viewed from a wider area of critical perspectives and interests than the one it had been immediately based upon. There is thus no reason why a certain critical procedure, which is not entirely incompatible with the indigenous critical canon, and which has proved to be a valuable technique elsewhere, may not be fruitfully applied to Indian Classical drama.

Viewed from the perspective of traditional Sanskrit criticism, a character such as Chanakya in *Mudra Rakshasam* can be described only as a *dhiroddhatta* character prepared in a heroic mode. His awe-inspiring personality, his terrible irascibility and his inscrutable mind would be the elements under focus. In the process, theatrical grandeur and dominance of the character would receive the greater critical attention. On the other hand, a free analysis would also concentrate on some of the apparently casual, discursive material in the play, and light upon significant, crucial relations and perspectives that would otherwise have been missed. In the process, it is not simply the character, but the experience of the play as a whole, which would be better understood.

Unlike characters in Kalidasa or Bhasa who are much more rounded, complex, and mulit-dimensional, Visakhadatta's are allegedly 'flat' in the Forsterian sense, despite being imbued with compelling dramatic power. But Visakhadatta is a great creative artist who does not fail to plumb the depths. Although his dramatic approach appears to be strictly determined by considerations of immediate theatricality, and although the subject of his play makes his dramatic *Karya* and *vibhavas* operate in a circumscribed space, he is able to produce complex characters whose outer bearings and inner feelings cannot be reduced to a simple equation. Chanakya, as the play reveals, is essentially a noble, selfless character. His political ruthlessness and wile which are for the greater part emphasised in the play in conformity with tradition keep conceated his generous self-denying disposition. The deft portrayal of his complex personality – as also those of others in the play – is likely to receive a fuller explication through Western methods of practical criticism than the conventional Indian approaches to *vibhava*.

Ancient Indian literary criticism, in certain ways marvellously close and exhaustive, does not really provide an adequate, revealing apparatus[18] for modern use. While it is true that indiscriminate application of Western norms (as, for instance, the Unities, social orientation or realism) on Indian Classical drama can be just perverse, some of their approaches could certainly be discriminatingly adopted with profit. One may thus make close studies of theme and imagery in order to achieve a fuller critical appreciation of the Sanskrit plays. It could, of course, be objected that Sanskrit canonists have already furnished well-calibrated theoretical apparatuses and that the precision which practical criticism wishes to achieve is already secured by the rigorous designing of the Classical plays. Practical criticism, the argument might thus run, is useful in the context of a drama which has greater ambivalence and complexity than the Indian plays. It might be claimed that the *sahridaya* and the playwright are already so thoroughly in agreement on the various aspects of dramatic composition that there is nothing left to 'discover'.

The intransigence of some Indian scholars in the matter of admitting Western critical approaches, therefore, is not altogether inexplicable. Thus, for example, Braj Vallabh Sharma in the Preface to his book on Bhavabhuti[19], avowedly prepared as a thoroughgoing exercise in traditional Sanskrit criticism, asserts that Indian Classical criticism is comprehensive enough to render all other imported critical modes not merely superflous, but misleading. The best illumination of Sanskrit drama, he claims, is possible only with torches handed down to us by Sanskrit canonists. With this convication he goes forward to discuss Bhavabhuti's plays along perspectives enunciated by traditional Sanskrit commentators. His performance is satisfactory, indeed, revealing through nearly two hundred and seventy pages of critical explication the close-knit structure, poetic beauties and blemishes, qualities of character, and other dramatic elements in Bhavabhuti. But, it is significant to note, with all this critical competence he does not really succeed in conveying a sufficiently intimate experience of the plays.

Since the higher form of Sanskrit drama did not have an orientation towards social criticism and concentrated on the more universal emotive-aesthetic components of *rasa*, and since Sanskrit theoreticians did not formulate a dramatic pattern conducive to the projection of metaphysical or moral complexity, one might feel discouraged to explore its thematic and symbolic patterns. But whenever a human story is dramatised – be it in the interest of *rasa* or character – various kinds of subtle interactions inevitably take place. The main deficiency of traditional Sanskrit commentaries relates to this area. Complacent over the comprehensiveness of ancient critical methods, the Sanskrit commentators usually do not consider it necessary to read between the lines or go beyond the immediate text to relate it to broad patterns of theme and image. Thus in the context of Bhavabhuti's play, not the moral conflict in Rama, but his emotional state alone, comes for emphasis. Not the mythical, dream-world atmosphere, but the reality of the situation and the sentiments of the protagonist become the focal points of criticism. While nature and setting as *uddipana vibhavas* are studied, the magical quality is taken for granted. The conservative critic, however thorough, does not either understand, or seek to amplify, the significance of the mythical, pastoral, dream-world atmosphere in *Uttara Ramacharitam*, and consequently misses a central perspective of the play, a point that will be clear when one compares Sharma's study with Wells' essay. [20]

But what, precisely, of Western criticism is likely to be useful in this context? One does not, surely, think of systematically applying to Indian Classical drama all the major approaches of dramatic criticism that have attained respectability in Europe. It is only obvious that because of certain fundamental historical and aesthetic differences between the two traditions, an outright, mechanical application of exotic methods and norms is likely to be critically pernicious. All healthy syncretism is gradual, selective, and slow-paced. To start with, then, some of the New-Critical procedures that have proved so revealing in the context of

Shakespearian studies, may be judiciously inducted to provide a helpful complement to Sanskrit criticism. It is necessary to remember here that Sanskrit criticism itself has a very respectable, long-standing tradition of *explication de texte.* It is rich in semantic and theoretical analyses, and has an extensive record of critical discussion pertaining to irony, symbolisation and metaphorical evocation. T. G. Mainkar[21] shows how rich the commentaries by Raghababhatta, Jayaddhara, Tripurari, Ghanashyama, Dhundiraja and others are in these respects.

Although Mainkar makes an extreme claim that these critics have practically done everything that a critic is expected to do[22], what may still be found wanting is a deeper thematic and psychological correlation to reveal literary complexities in a text. Most of the theoretical studies confine themselves to certain set illustrations, as did the older treatises; and most of the commentaries on literary texts are engaged in the identification of *rasa, alankaras, chhanda* etc, besides furnishing lexical annotation. The focus being constantly kept on certain schematised psychological elements and general aesthetic features, the essential individuality of a work of art and its subtler methods of structural and thematic organisation which practical criticism so cogently reveals are not spelt out in most of these celebrated commentaries. A number of Indian critics[23] in modern times have noted this particular deficiency in traditional Sanskrit criticism. But a corresponding awareness of the responsibility for correcting the imbalance, and undertaking extended discussions of literary texts along modern lines has not been much in evidence.

Western interest in Sanskrit literature has been welcomed as a liberating and vitalising influence. To the traditional Indian critics it came as some kind of a revelation, and acquired remarkable critical authority. But its contribution was chiefly in the realms of literary history and documentation. An examination of the history of Western literary-critical studies, their successes and failures, is particularly instructive in this context.

One may begin an account of Western criticism on Indian Classical plays with H. H. Wilson whose *Theatre of the Hindus* was the first to attempt a comprehensive study of the subject. Written in the third decade of the nineteenth century, Wilson's account of *Hindu* drama – a competent work of scholarship for those days – betrays an understandable critical difficulty. He is one of the pioneers in Europe to attempt a full-length study of Sanskrit drama, and this naturally ties him down, for the most part, to the business of historical survey and technical exposition. His book contains just a few pages of literary criticism proper. Paucity of critical material at his disposal might also have been responsible for his sketchy approach. Whatever be the reasons, we find Wilson quite content to pass a few summary judgements on the Indian plays and rounding off his study. Clearly, he feels no urge to tackle the plays with some degree of critical thoroughness. And, more unfortunately, he is prone to making loose generalisations. For instance, Schlegel's comment on the 'romantic' quality of *Abhijnana* becomes in his hands a comprehensive description of the entire body of Indian drama. Thus he begins by commenting:[24]

> Indian criticism, however, has been always in its infancy. It never learned to connect causes and effects. It never looked to the influence exercised by imagination or passion in poetry; it never, in short, became either poetical or philosophical.

That this judgement reveals a basic incomprehension of the modality and purpose of ancient Indian drama is only too obvious. However, this does not deter the Indian reader all at once; for, such a prefatory announcement naturally builds an anticipation of a more productive critical attempt in the book to join 'causes and effects', and to furnish some 'poetical', 'philosophical' appreciation in the manner of, say, Dryden and Coleridge. The sense of disappointment, however, becomes acute when Wilson is found engaging in merely sociological and historical discussion. The chapter on *Mudra Rakshasam* has eighteen pages[25] of writing on Chandragupta's historical identity to a mere page-long[26] literary observation, half of which, again, is usurped by a tirade against the 'curious' state of public morals in ancient India. Similarly, the chapter on *Mrichchakatikam* is an extended discussion of dubious value on some socio-political questions, with only a page of undistinguished critical observation tagged at the end. Wilson's limitations are, in fact, already in evidence before he has come to an examination of the plays proper. In a chapter discussing characterisation, his rather superficial and prejudiced approach to the question is rendered obvious when, instead of examining Vasantasena's character, he dilates on the question of the status of Indian women and concludes by making the following 'critical' observation[27]:

> In practice, however, greater latitude seems to have been observed; and in the *Mrichchakati* a Brahman, a man of family and repute, incurs apparently no discredit for his love for a courtesan. A still more curious feature is that his passion for such an object seems to excite no sensation in his family nor uneasiness in his wife, and the nurse presents his child to his mistress, as to its mother; and his wife, besides interchanging civilities (a little coldly, perhaps,

> but not compulsively) finishes by calling her, "sister", and acquiescing therefore in the legal union with her husband.

As we shall see, there could hardly be a more obtuse reading of the story of Vasantsena and Charudatta.

The four or five pages of literary-critical discussion available in Wilson's book contain only a few conventional observations derived from certain traditional Western concepts like dramatic unities, verisimilitude, and tragic plot. Wilson's appreciation at all points cannot, by any means, be viewed as wilfully prejudiced or uninformed; but even though mostly it steers clear of the two extremes and keeps to a common-sense approach, it never attains to the quality of perceptive literary criticism. *The Theatre of the Hindus*, then, is a useful document to illustrate the aesthetic difficulty of the average nineteenth-century Western reader of Indian drama, and not one to demonstrate a fruitful transplantation of Western sensibility on the Indian soil. Had Wilson devoted himself uninhibitedly to the task of critical evaluation, his achievement would have been more salutary. As it happened, employing a few narrowly conventional notions he offered a criticism which was useful only in a negative sense – to work as a warning and not an inspiration.

For the next specialised study on the corpus of ancient Sanskrit drama to appear Europe had to wait till the last decade of the nineteenth century. In terms of amplitude and critical sympathy, Professor Sylvain Levi's thesis, published under the title *The Theatre of India*, has had very few peers in Western criticism of Indian drama[28]. The inclusiveness and ardour of his approach are borne out by the introductory remarks:

> Once the essential features of the Indian drama are thus established, one may set out to find their underlying principle. We have studied analytically the personages, the emotions, the action and the language of the drama; we have then shown the logical concatenation of the various parts; finally, we have attempted a synthesis. The taste for idealized emotions and for suggested sentiments gives a ready explanation of the creation and development of the laws which regulate the dramatic art. And this naturally leads us to the fundamental principle of the Indian genius. And such has been the final objective of our research. It was not the quest for a mere literary enjoyment which prompted us to undertake the study of the Indian theatre and to spend long years in the analysis. The technical precepts of Bharata, Dhananjaya and Vishvanatha together with the innumerable dramatic productions do not give us a more refined relish of Kalidasa's delicate sensibility, of Bhavabhuti's moving pathos, of Sudraka's spirited vitality, of Harsa's poetic precision, but they give a pleasure to the spirit which surpasses all the charm of the most beautiful verse. They introduce us to one of the strangest, strongest and most

> original geniuses which contributed to the growth of civilization. It is the history of the Indian genius which we have undertaken to retrace.

Levi has many perspective comments to offer. But while his comprehensive approach and love of the subject produce excellent critical results, he is still far from achieving a proper understanding of the position of the Classical Sanskrit dramatist. As a consequence, leaning heavily upon traditional Western preferences, he often blunders into startling generalisations.[29] This was possibly natural at that point of time, and it does not detract from the importance of Levi's achievement, But it is instructive to see how a 'European' predilection for realistic, verisimilar delineation affects his judgement all through the book. Realising fully well the beauties of symbolic stylization in Indian drama, Levi yet finds it difficult to free himself from 'realistic' preoccupations. This manifests itself variously at a number of points in his study.

Sometimes it may have as general a reference as the unity of time: 'The seven Acts follow one another without the least solution of continuity'[30]. Or it may relate to the management of dramatic introduction: 'The whole approach is childish: the director conveniently informs the public of everything that happens between the various incidents'[31].Elsewhere his extreme absorption in concepts of realistic 'imitation' finds pointed expression – 'The historical argument based on the assumption that the drama reflects the customs of the time and place where it was composed has little value. We already drew the attention to this in the case of *Malavikagnimitra.* Indian society never resembled the picture drawn in *Mrichchakatika*... We are, as in the rest of the Indian theatre, in complete convention, in complete fantasy'[32]. These find an inevitable summing-up in the followings remarks:[33]

> The Indian Muse has dissociated the drama from real life and created an imaginary society on the model of Brahmanic society with no danger on the part of the audience to mistake it for reality. Hence the spectator can abandon himself without fear to the enjoyment of emotions which he knows belong to another world.

It would be wrong to condemn Levi on the strength of present-day ideas on the relationship between the real and the stylised in literature. But even under more traditional schemes, as are, for instance, adumbrated in Shakespeare's romances, a good deal of what Levi thinks exceptionable in Indian drama should have appeared more acceptable and admirable. Levi's commitment to realism, however, is too deep to facilitate a more enlightened aesthetic response to the plays. This makes him oblivious not only of the nature of reality in the Indian drama but also of the quality of its *rasa*-organisation. Thus we have comments such as the following.[34]

> Actually the *Mrchhakatika* is nothing but a popular story divided into scenes and treated in the Indian manner with a plethora of incidents and episodes. The poet has used the ordinary method of filling the ten acts corresponding to the ten division of the action with lyrical and descriptive stanzas.

> The *Uttara Ramacharita* is less a drama than a series of scenes, some lyrical, some descriptive. Bhavabhuti had selected a certain number of scenes and loosely joined them together....

One may pass over some other well-known European commentators on Indian drama before and after – Pischel, Klein, Winternitz, Harrowitz, and others – and move on to A. A. Macdonell's *A History of Sanskrit Literature*[35] which provides a relatively more sustained literary-critical appreciation of individual Sanskrit plays. It is possible to glean from the others a variety critical observations interesting, debatable or erroneous – but they are mostly preoccupied with background matters or historical issues and do not carry one much beyond Wilson and Levi in terms of critical sensibility. They may have, here and there, some interesting insights to offer, but since these are not derived from, nor designed to stimulate, any extended critical studies of the plays, the interest is merely of a localised, incidental kind. Unlike most of his predecessors, however, Macdonell does not get engrossed in merely historical discussion and is eager to go beyond the summary of a play. Bound as he is to the constraints of a historical survey, he yet keeps his focus squarely on the individual plays, and in a compact essay of about twenty pages, furnishes a number of pointed remarks and fresh generalisations. To the extent that he treats the plays as objects of serious critical attention, and not as mere illustrations of some preconceived notions on Indian drama, his effort is commendable.

He does not, it is true, achieve any extraordinary success in projecting the essential beauty of the Sanskrit drama. He commits quite a few critical misjudgments in respect of genre, plot and character, but not necessarily because the plays represent an alien tradition. Even things which could have been understood with relatively greater accuracy on the basis of conventions available to the ancient Western theatre are also erroneously viewed. Thus his statement that the Sanskrit dramatists do not show much fertility of inventions, commonly borrowing the story of their plays from history or epic legend[36], is a surprising criticism to come from one acquainted with the Greek and Elizabethan dramatic achievements. With all his failings, however, Macdonell can be said to have successfully advanced the possibilities of critical interaction between Western and Indian sensibilities. His comment on Kalidasa is illustrative:[37]

> The richness of creative fancy he displays in these, and his skill in the expression of tender feeling, assign him a high place among the dramatists of the world. The harmony of the poetic sentiment is nowhere disturbed by anything violent or terrifying. Every passion is softened without being enfeebled. The ardour of love never goes beyond aesthetic bounds; it never maddens to wild jealousy or hate. The torments of sorrow are toned down to a profound and touching melancholy. It was here at last that the Indian genius found the law of moderation in poetry, which it hardly knew elsewhere and thus produced works of enduring beauty. Hence it was that *Shakuntala* exercised so great a fascination on the calm intellect of Goethe, who at the same time was so strongly repelled by the extravagances of Hindu mythological art.

The application of a refined Western sensibility introduces here a value and a perspective not easy to develop on the basis of traditional Sanskrit commentaries. But such passages in Macdonell are too few to have set in motion any major alteration of sensibility.

From Macdonell one is naturally conveyed to his pupil, Alexander Barridale Keith, whose critical acumen was already being praised by Macdonell in the preface to his book in 1899. The publication of Keith's *The Sanskrit Drama* in 1924 is a major event in the history of Western appreciation of Indian dramatic literature. Both scholarly and critical in its orientation, it constitutes the first extended Western study of Indian drama designed to concentrate in a balanced manner on historical-technical issues and on literary appreciation. Most earlier writings had leaned too heavily towards historical, descriptive assays, and had offered only brief critical remarks – in passing, as it were. Their literary pronouncements were, therefore, likely to be rather pontifical in tone, and summary in style. It had seemed as if Indian drama did not appeal to its Western critics as a potential material for extended critical discussion; since they could not discern much complexity or profundity in the Indian drama, they thought it was enough to indicate certain of its merits and deficiencies in broad general terms and pass on to sociological and historical issues. In this context Keith's appearance marks a major point of transition: he not only seeks to present an account of the history and formal design of Indian drama, but also comes forward with a more detailed discussion of individual plays than had been hitherto attempted.

That Keith is not always able to command an unprejudiced approach to his subject should not cause surprise or generate the suspicion that it is a case of wilful perversity. While evaluating his work today, it is necessary for the critic to develop an understanding of, and sympathy for, his historical position. The then state of cultural interaction between England and India was bound to leave its impress on Keith's study, and some of the things which could have appeared fair and legitimate to him at that stage of Oriental studies, might seem today somewhat quaint and even preposterous. His thesis in chapter XII linking Sanskrit drama to what he reads as ancient Brahmanical values, may be taken as an example:[38]

> The drama bears, therefore, essential traces of its connection with the Brahmans. They are.... capable of large generalisations, but regardless of accuracy in detail.
>
> The emotions which thus it was desired to evoke were, however, strictly limited by the Brahmanical theory of life.

While, however, all such sociological correlations in his book may not be construed as baseless or inept, the kind of conclusions to which they lead him would produce an impression that Keith is not in sympathy with the Indian aesthetic position. His is, once again, the average European mind which believed that, between Sophocles and Shakespeare, all the higher possibilities of the dramatic form had been exhausted.

It is not as if Keith entirely fails to appreciate the difference between the aesthetic preconceptions of Western and Sanskrit dramas. But one of the basic elements which he does not seem to have adequately grasped is the profound psychological-emotional import of *rasa* at the artistic level. He appears to be too much an admirer of the Western dramatic values to be able to sympathetically investigate the essential merits of Indian dramatic theory. He writes:[39]

The accurate delineation of facts or character to them was nothing; they aimed at the creation of sentiment in the mind of the audience, and what was necessary for this end was all that was attempted.

To a Western theatre-goer who confines himself to standard notions of 'sentiment' in relation to *rasa*, and thinks of the *alambana* and *uddipana vibhavas* as some conventional tools mechanically used in support of the 'sentiment', Sanskrit drama is bound to appear facile. From such a position, it is rather inevitable that judgements such as the following should emerge:

> It follows..... that the plot is a secondary element in the drama in its highest form... The Nataka.[40]

> Limited by the nature of the intellectual movement which produced it, the Sanskrit drama could never achieve the perfection of great tragedy or comedy. Kalidasa, the greatest Indian dramatist, expresses no uneasiness at the structure of life or the working of the world.[41]

> Fascinating and exquisite as is the *Sakuntala* it moves in a narrow world, removed far from the cruelty of real life, and it neither seeks to answer, nor does it solve, the riddles of life. Bhavabhuti, it is true, shows some sense of the complexity and difficulty of existence but with him also.... all must end in harmony.[42]

Even if Indian Classical drama were all that Keith supposes it to be, why 'uneasiness' should necessarily constitute a more exciting dramatic value and a profounder philosophical position than 'serenity' is difficult to understand, unless, of course, one is already committed to the faith that Greek and Elizabethan dramatic values alone are respectable. The extent to which Keith is determined to prove the impossibility of sustaining higher forms of tragic drama in the Indian Classical theatre becomes evident when he confronts a play like *Urubhangam* with all the ingredients of a tragedy, and something more besides. Keith's assertion that *Urubhangam* which has erroneously been treated as a tragedy (Luders being "responsible for the view that Duryodhan is the hero")[43] and that Duryodhana is the chief subject, but not the hero, of the piece which manifests the just punishment of the impious'[44] shows his reluctance to grant even a passing success of the Western kind to an Indian play.

For all his errors of emphasis and contention, however, Keith's devotion to the task of critical exposition is admirable. He succeeds in making a good many penetrating observations on Sanskrit drama on the strength of this intellectual sincerity. But the more significant aspect of his work should have been the projection of a new critical style. Had his criticism more directly involved the free exercise of an eclectic Western sensibility, it would have, notwithstanding the lapse already alluded to, attained a truly classical status. It should then have paved the way for a more comprehensive and liberal appreciation of Indian drama. As it stands, Keith's effort is largely confined to a mechanical application of certain traditional Western concepts on the Sanskrit plays. He is hardly disturbed by the thought that many of these concepts may be utterly untenable in the context of the Oriental theatre. If, instead of concentrating on those conventional questions Keith had simply adopted the Western procedure of critical analysis while maintaining a proper respect for the fundamental values of the Indian tradition, his revaluation of Sanskrit drama would have been a great deal more satisfying. But his approach is normative, rather than comparative, and hence does not bring about an enrichment of critical understanding.

Most other Western critics of Sanskrit drama display a similar lack of sympathy with the Indian point of view. And, hence, what could have furnished a new stimulus to Indian critics served only the spurious purpose of encouraging misguided criticism. Against this background, H. W. Wells' book, the *Classical Drama of India* offers an exciting critical experience. It brings into play a rich comparative perspective, and presents certain reassessments of Indian Classical drama with brilliant insight and understanding. This is not to say that the contributions of critics like Macdonell, and Keith are unimportant or of slight consequence. But their studies do not show a real warmth of appreciation, a sense of true communion and fresh adventure. While, therefore, many of their scholarly statements are illuminating, their literary-critical pronouncements are of a mediocre quality in most cases. Wells not merely understands the Indian position exceedingly well, he also knows how his predecessors went wrong.[45]

This, of course, does not make his own criticism entirely fool-proof. One finds him saying, for instance, 'It is scarcely a misrepresentation to state that most of the heroines are little more than privileged members of a herem'[46]. Such startling assertions are, however, few and far between. By and large Wells' literary appreciation remains free of cultural prejudice, and his writings triumphantly demonstrate the critical importance of the exercise of a liberal Western sensibility on Indian Classical drama.

Occasional lapses that occur in Wells, one tends to feel, may be glossed over because of the aesthetic thrill which pervades the entire body of his writing. His mind may be Western, but when he reads Indian drama it is with the heart, reassuringly, of a *sahridaya.* As has been already suggested, such a combination was precisely what had been lacking in most European studies in Indian drama. It is however necessary to point out that Wells by himself is not the complete answer to the problem of criticism projected here. Although his is a sensitive and illuminating study, his critical pronouncements could have been more controlled, and less elusive, than they are. Wells' is a general introduction, a most competent and stimulating one, to be sure, but many of its insights and suggestions still remain to be worked out and tested. Some of his comments are like brilliant flashes of lightning, revealing and concealing at the same time. The vision thus available needs to be more steadily and comprehensively figured forth and illustrated with reference to the corpus of Sanskrit plays. Wells' argument is circumscribed by the space at his disposal, as also by the focus on broad features and final impressions. Similarly generalised are his prefatorial comments in *Six Sanskrit plays*[47]. An extended application of the techniques of practical criticism is still being awaited in the field of Sanskrit drama.

The following essays seek to explore possibilities of fresh analysis. The effort is to bring out patterns of theme, motif and characterisation along modern lines of critical enquiry without ignoring the special aesthetic and cultural milieu implicit in the plays. Critical concepts from both European and Indian traditions have been freely introduced, but without engaging in an amplification of comparative aesthetics or of technical details, so that the main focus is unremittingly kept on critical elucidation of the texts proper. While broad aesthetic principles have been referred to, no pauses are taken to elaborate upon theoretical aspects. Certain comparative statements on the relative positions of the two dramatic traditions are offered with only a practical, literary-critical bias. It is hoped, once the danger of false analogues and sweeping generalisations is avoided, a synthetic approach connecting both the traditions would be critically far more revealing than specialised, insulated perspectives confined to any of them.

Chapter One takes up the question of *rasa-synthesis* in *Abhijnana Shakuntalam*, which in a sense represents the consummation of Sanskrit dramatic tradition. It tries to throw into relief the inadequacy of conventional approaches by freshly examining an element which traditional Sanskrit criticism should be ordinarily expected to competently handle. Discussing the nature of the critical deficiency in European and Indian approaches to the play, the essay seeks to demonstrate how a proper appreciation of Classical Sanskrit drama today demands an integrated, discriminating use of both Western practical criticism and Sanskrit poetics. It argues that traditional studies on the play which concentrate on *shringara* as its *angirasa* fail to do justice to the creative vision of Kalidasa. While the central importance of *shringara* is not denied, on the basis of a close reading of the text an attempt is made to reveal how it attains a marvellous, unique kind of enlargement through a concurrently unswerving concentration on *vatsala*.

Chapter Two takes up for study Shudraka's *Mrichchakatikam*, which in terms of theme and sensibility is reputed to be particularly germane to modern taste. An attempt is made to show how the play is neither predominantly realistic, as is universally claimed, nor is it merely a conventionally stylised, poetic piece. An exposition of the splendid comprehensiveness of Shudraka's vision is attempted through a study of the various thematic undercurrents encountered in the play. The major point of discussion relates to the dramatic synthesis of a number of dualities and dichotomies which go to impart an inclusive, 'Shakespearian' character to the play.

Chapter Three examines Bhavabhuti's *Uttara Ramacharitam*, a play that stands unsurpassed in terms of the intensity of *karuna rasa*. The essay attempts to offer a fresh view of Bhavabhuti's dramatic design and tries to relate major questions on the play to a controlling pattern that shapes it. It also attempts to set in proper perspective one of the most closely debated issues concerning the play, namely, its ethical vision.

Chapter Four seeks to demonstrate how dramatic poetry and characterisation in Visakhadatta's *Mudra Rakshasam* function in a complex, multivalent style, with nothing of the stereotyped and unidimensional character alleged against them. The analysis is meant to highlight Visakhadatta's remarkable dramatic control, and his concern for a broad human appeal which manifests itself engagingly through the poetry and characters of the play.

Chapter Five discusses Bhasa's originality of approach to the business of dramatic organisation. It analyses a play which is famous for its violation of Bharata's injunction against representation of death of the hero on the stage, and takes issue with critics, Western and Indian, who have gone on discussing it as a tragedy. Bhasa was both traditional and innovative in his approach. The essay tries to argue how Bhasa made a radical departure from convention by portraying death of the hero, but so contrived the play that it should intensify, not grief or loss, but exaltation and serenity, and thus conform to the Classical norm while apparently moving away from it.

Together, the essays attempt an extended revaluation of Classical Sanskrit drama, seeking to stimulate critical rethinking of a comprehensive kind on the subject. The tradition is examined from a wide variety of perspectives. Genre, character, *rasa*, dramatic organisation, theme, cultural values, dramatic poetry, and vision of human life, are some of the aspects discussed with reference to five of the most exquisite creations of the Indian theatre.

Notes and References

1. See, R.C.Majumdar and A.D. Pusalker (ed.), *The History and Culture of the Indian People,* Vol-II, Bharatiya Vidya Bhavan, Bombay, 1951; *The Cultural Heritage of India*, Vol.II, Ramakrishna Mission Institute of Culture, Calcutta, 1962 (Chapters XVI, XXV, XXVII, XXVIII, XXIX, and XXXI, in particular, provide a revealing picture of the fundamental changes taking place in the social, ethical and political spheres during the Maurya and Gupta periods); and U.N. Ghosal, *A History of Indian Political Ideas*, Oxford University Press, 1966.
2. See, D.D.Kosambi, *The Culture and Civilisation of Ancient India in Historical Outline*, Vikas Publishing House Pvt Ltd., Delhi, 1970; Romila Thapar, *A History of India,* Vol. I, Penguin Books, 1966; K.Damodaran, *Indian Thought: A Critical History,* Asia Publishing House, Bombay, 1967; and, Debi Prasad Chattopadhyaya, *Lokayata,* People's Publishing House, Delhi, Third Edition, 1973. Some scholars (for example, S.R.Goyal, 'The Future of Research in Ancient Indian History', *Indica,* September 1977, Vol. 14, No.2, pp. 85-99) plead for a total rejection of European approaches to historiography, but these are particularly important for the student of literature who is concerned with a set of comprehensive, universal human values, and not with specific national perspectives.
3. For example, *Mahakavi Bhasa* by Dr. Nemichand Sastri (Madhya Pradesh Hindi Grantha Academy, Bhopal, 1972), is planned ambitiously, extending over 565 pages, but has nothing new to offer by way of critical appreciation.
4. Indu She3khar, *Sanskrit Drama: Its Origin and Decline,* Leiden, 1959.
5. Ayodhya Prasad Singh, *Bhavabhuti Aur Unki Natyakala,* Motilal Banarasidess, Delhi, 1969.
6. Dwijendra Lal Ray, *Kalidas Aur Bhavabhuti,* Second Edition, Hindi Grantha Ratnakar Pvt. Ltd., Bombay, 1956.
7. For a sample, see, R.C.Knight (ed.) *Racine (Modern Judgements),* Macmillan & Co., 1969.
8. Leo Aylen, *Greek Tragedy and the Modern World*, Methuen & Co., London, 1964.
9. John Jones, *On Aristotle and Greek Tragedy,* London, 1962; shows how a number of commentators on Aristotle have modified his emphasis on *action* and have effected an unwarranted primacy of *character.*
10. Laxmi Narayan Lal, *Rangamancha Aur Nataka Ki Bhumika,* National Publishing House, Delhi, 1974.
11. K.C.Pandey, *Comparative Aesthetics,* Vol. I, Chowkhamba Sanskrit Studies Series, 1959.
12. Acharya Valadev Upadhyaya, *Bharatiya Sahitya Sastra,* Third Edition, Nandakishore and Sons, Varanasi, 1967; particularly the concluding portions discussing "Aucitya" and "Vakrokti" from a comparative standpoint.
13. G.B.Mohan, *The Response to Poetry*, People's Publishing House, Delhi, 1968.
14. R.N. Singhal, *Aristotle and Bharata*, n.p., 1977; a lucid, comprehensive introduction to the fundamental tenets of Poetics and Natya Sastra, but not very illuminating

in terms of critical comparison; in his essay, "A comparative study of the Sanskrit and the Greek Dramatic theory", P.L. Bhargava *Principles of Literary Criticism in Sanskrit*, Ed. R.C.Dwivedi, Motilal Bariarsidass, Delhi, 1969) shows the same kind of limitation.

15. See, Henry W. Wells and H.H.Anniah Gowda, *Style and Structure in Shakespeare*, Vikas Publishing House Pvt. Ltd., Delhi, 1979. In the essay, "Othello and Rasadhvani theory" (Chapter XV) they develop a comparison between *Othello* and *Uttara Ramacharitam* based on the obvious similarity of the heroines' undeserved suffering. But, Desdemona and Sita are treated much too differently, and the plays breathe much too different atmospheres, to make the comparison really meaningful. The basic question of the nature of the *rasa* in *Othello*, would bring home the untenability of such a critical identification.

16. Greek drama, too, placed an unremitting focus on character. But, whereas the Greek dramatist placed a great deal of emphasis on the Chorus and made use of character as a medium for the exploration of moral or spiritual values, thus rendering it essentially secondary, Racine's interest was primarily focussed on passion. In this respect he is unique in the Western theatre- world.

17. A.B.Keith, *The Sanskrit Drama*, Oxford University Press, Reprinted 1970, p.280:

    "Kalidasa, the greatest of Indian dramatists expresses no uneasiness at the structure of life or the working of the world."

    To this we might oppose the more perceptive comment by S.K.De:

    "His tranquillity, considered as an attitude towards life, is not easy-going indifference or placid acquiescence in the order of things; there is enough of earnestness and sense of sorrow to indicate that it must have been hard won, although we are denied the sight of the strife and struggle which led to its attainment,"...

    S.N.Dasgupta and S.K.De, A History of Sanskrit Literature, Vol. I, Second Edition, University of Calcutta, 1977, p. 152.

18. This has been recognised and commented upon by modem writers on Sanskrit literature, but to no material purpose, for it has not led to any significant realignment of critical perspectives. See, Ramji Upadhyaya, *Sanskrita Sahitya Ka Alochanatmaka Itihasa*, Part I, Ramnanrayan Venimadhab, Allahabad, 1970. In the *Foreword* to the book Dr. Upadhyaya writes:

    It appears as if literary criticism could hardly go beyond the taste and predilection of the "nagaraka". Modern critics have to pay attention to this, and guide the new writers by broadening the scope of criticism. The critic has to suggest the design of literature which is intended to build spiritual, moral and metaphysical edifices of a nation.

    But the book hardly ever fulfils the expectations it raises with such statements. The last sentence shows how a misguided literary programme is envisaged on the basis of a 'modern' taste.

19. Braj Vallabh Sharma, *Bhavabhuti Ke Natak*, Madhya Pradesh Hindi Grantha Academy, Bhopal, 1973.

20. Henry W. Wells, *The Classical Drama of India*, Ch. XIII, Asia Publishing House, Delhi, 1963.
21. T.G.Mainkar, *Studies in Sanskrit Dramatic Criticism,* Motilal Banarasidass, Delhi, 1977.
22. Ibid, p. 113.
23. "Sanskrit Poetics cannot explain satisfactorily, for instance, the simple question as to why the work of one poet is not the same in character as that of another, or why two works of the same poet are not the same" – S.N.Dasgupta and S.K.De, op. cit., p. 29. In a similar strain. Ram Chandra Prasad (*Literary Criticism in Hindi*, Sarita Prakasan, Meerut, 1976 – p. 11) discusses this deficiency of Sanskrit Criticism. V.K.Gokak, similarly, lists "four important things (which) Indian aesthetics learnt from the European contact" (The Concept of Indian Literature, Munshiram Manoharlal, Delhi, 1979, p. 160). Few works showing a fruitful application of this 'learning' on Sanskrit drama are, however, available.
24. H.H.Wilson, et al, *The Theatre of the Hindus*, Indological Book House, Delhi, u.d., p.4.
25. Ibid., pp. 75-92.
26. Ibid., pp. 92-93.
27. Ibid., p. 29.
28. Sylvain Levi, *The Theatre of India,* Vol. I, pp. 8-9, Narayan Mukherji (Trans.), Writer's Workshop, Calcutta, 1978.
29. Ibid., p. 6:

    "We have resolutely left aside the question of style. The drama does not possess a style of its own."

    Again, Ibid., Vol. II, pp. 126-7:

    "The Nataka.... finds its integration in dance. The Greek drama is the action itself.... Weakened by the climate, crushed by an overwhelming nature which surrounds him, he (the Indian) gives up a fight which he knows to be unequal......."
30. Ibid., Vol. I, p. 150 (on *Abhijnana Shakuntalam*).
31. Ibid., Vol. I, p. 156 (on *Abhijnana Shakuntalam*).
32. Ibid., Vol. I, p. 179 (on *Mrichchakatika*)
33. Ibid., vol. II, pp. 121-2.
34. Ibid., Vol. I, p. 181 & p. 199.
35. A.A.Macdonell, *A History of Sanskrit Literature*, Second Indian Edition, Motilal Banarasidass, Delhi, 1971 (First Published – 1899).
36. Ibid., p. 195.
37. Ibid., p. 298.
38. A.B.Keith, *The Sanskrit Drama*, Oxford University Press, 1970, Reprint), pp. 276-7.
39. Ibid., p. 276.
40. Ibid., p. 277.

41. Ibid., p. 280.
42. Ibid., p. 281.
43 Ibid., p. 38.
44. Ibid., p. 106.
45. Henry W. Wells, op. cit., p. 2:

    "His (Keith's) defect is partly owing to commitment to British Morality but much more to a conservative view in aesthetics leading him to discover the norm for serious drama in Greek tragedy and the ultimate vision in theatrical opinion in the theories of Aristotle.... Keith approached Indian drama and poetry with an analytical mind but a cold heart."
46. Ibid., p. 84.
47. Henry W. Wells, *Six Sanskrit Plays*, Asia Publishing House, Delhi, 1964.

CHAPTER 2

Abhijnana Shakuntalam: Rasa Synthesis

Kalidasa was one of the most disciplined of writers, and even ordinary details in his plays were endowed with a clear dramatic purpose. And he wrote for an alert, cultivated body of *sahridayas* who were familiar with the sophisticated stylisations so meticulously documented in Bharata's *Natyashastra.* In keeping with the critical tradition, therefore, his masterpiece should be expected to engage an unequivocal, preponderant *angi-rasa*, the principal aesthetic emotion of a *Kavya.* It was thus natural that most readers of *Abhijnana Shakuntalam* should have responded to the play in terms of the classically defined *shringara rasa*, relegating every other element to the conventional position of subsidiaries. Few, if ever, have sought to cut through the settled stereotypes of critical habit and looked for more complex patterns of symbolisation. The rich sophistication that has gone into the making of the play seems to have, in different ways, inhibited fresh critical thinking among both Indian and European scholars.

The kind of difficulties that might beset an average European's appreciation of *Abhijnana* have been touched upon – in passing – by a number of Indian critics. More significantly, certain careful attempts at expounding the aesthetic barrier have also seen made[1]. Built upon a multitude of poetic nuances, and catering to an aesthetic which subordinates and orchestrates every other dramatic element to the creation of *rasa*, it is only natural that this play should seem elusive in certain respects to a mind steeped in social drama. Shudraka's *Mrichchakatikam* has had thus a greater appeal for the European mind. He can always understand it better[2]. His predilection for melodrama[3], complex sexual passions, multiple plot, and realistic representation finds better scope here than in the relatively more rarefied and poetic atmosphere of *Abhijnana.* Further, the tragic mode which contrives the most captivating dramatic experience for the European being replaced here by a more harmonious and inclusive design catering to a state of serene joy, *Abhijnana* produces in him only the lesser appeal of a romance.

It is not as if *Abhijnana* – or Sanskrit drama in general, as we shall more fully examine in later chapters-averts its gaze from the spectacle of human suffering. But an unremitting and passionate dedication to a certain philosophy of joy controls its presentation of dramatic experience. This cannot really be understood in the manner of Anouilh's chorus[4] which wistfully, yet ironically, asserts the restfulness that comes with all passions spent, nor in terms of Frye's argument that there is a sense of comedy and grace at the heart of every great tragedy, the fine critical scope of which is extensively developed by Cyrus Hoy[5]. The serenity of Sanskrit *nataka* is not something that issues from conventional tragi-comic resolutions. Nor is it of a kind that reminds one of Aeschylean resolution or Sophoclean acceptance. It presupposes a more profound and comprehensive vision of the universe, and of man's place in it, as being ordered by an everlasting principle of joy. As an important corollary to this, elements of transgression and guilt in the main character, which are at the heart of European tragedy do not find favour in the Sanskrit *nataka*. The latter has for its justification an exact reverse of Nietzche's Dionysian ideal and its cathartic function.

In the case of certain other Sanskrit plays – a romantic tragi-comedy like Shudraka's *Mricchakatikam,* or a political play like Visakhadatta's *Mudra Rashasam* – an incomplete realisation of the spirit of this tradition and a less rigorous aesthetic discipline may not so greatly inhibit one's understanding and enjoyment as in the case of *Abhijnana*. The most sophisticated specimen of a *sukumara nataka*[6], composed in the *vaidarbhi riti*[7], it calls for close responsiveness to various shades of delicate, poetic suggestions and demands a constant awareness of the ancient Indian cultural mores and world-view. The importance of this discipline can be appreciated from the fact that even Indian critics have on occasions floundered on relaxing their attention.

We might turn to certain readings in the character of Shukuntala for an elucidation. The first thing we might note in this context is that she is not presented in just conventional terms. With all the typical features of a heroine prescribed by the *Natyashastra*, she is yet a richly individualised character endowed with a complex personality. A number of opposites such as grace and strength, innocence and maturity, modesty and pride, softness and severity, blend in her character and render her into one of the most captivating creations in world drama. As we shall see, critics who view her only through glasses handed down by Bharata falsify her as much as those who resort to Elizabethan perspectives, similar distortions occur with respect to her dramatic status, and to the theme for which she is the principal medium. Clearly, she is at the very centre of the play; but *Abhijana is not about her* in the same sense that Racine's *Pheadra*, for example, is about its heroine. Nor is the play itself a story of love, as such, with Shakuntala serving the purpose of just a romantic heroine. Kalidasa has, indeed proved himself one of the greatest sculptors of love. As Robert Antoine says[8]:

> He is supreme in depicting love. No one has ever conveyed with so great and delicate an art the first thrills of nascent love, the all-absorbing fascination of growing love, the exquisite torment of pining love and the unsurpassable bliss of fulfilled love.

But 'the interest of the *Shukuntala'* is not 'in the love of a woman's guileless heart'[9], as Mirashi and Navlekar emphasize. Had it been so, it could hardly attain the status of one of the greatest of Classical Sanskrit plays, catering to the goal of *Trivarga praptih*, as the *Natyashastra* would have it.

Both because of the special conditions governing her characterization and the uniqueness of the conception, Shakuntala as a character has no real parallel in Western drama. All the same, there is no dearth of comparative linkages, and the character of Miranda has come to be almost a standard footnote to discussions on Shakuntala. Unfortunately, however, such comparisons are often over-stretched or just casually mentioned. It is instructive to note how Tagore, who warned against simplistic generalisations on Miranda and Shakuntala as kindred personalities, himself got swayed by his 'poetic' reading of the play, as evidenced in the essay, 'Shakuntala', and its companion piece, 'Kumara Sambhava-O-Shakuntala'. Since Tagore's essays have served as seminal influences on later criticism, it is necessary to touch upon one or two of his views that illustrate the dangers inherent in too free an application of modern sensibility on the play.

As may be seen, the allegorical scheme which Tagore proposed, though very revealing and persuasive, also misleads at places because of its quality of emphasis. Thus, for example, he exaggerates the 'transgression' committed by the lovers, and takes Durbasa's curse as being merely metaphorical. Metaphorical the whole play is, and this need be no more metaphorical than the other elements. It is important to see that Kalidasa has been exceedingly careful to prevent a possible over-emphasis on the so-called transgression. Both the lovers are, of course, made to express the fear of violating the sanctity of the hermitage; it is, as Shakuntala says, *a tapovana virodhi vikara* which has her in its grip. But the characters are not conscious of, or represented as, doing anything evil. The question of *chastisement*, therefore, is out of place.[11] The very nature of this main characters, the essential purity and righteousness of both the lovers is, therefore, repeatedly emphasised in the play. Dushyanta is presented as a noble *Rajarshi*; he is so firmly established in virtue that he can more than once confidently declare his total freedom from base impulses[12]. Other characters, too, testify to his moral excellence, an interesting example being the case of the two young ascetics who visit him in Act II, and awed by his personality, refer to the appropriateness of calling him a sage king.[13]

But Tagore is forced by his thesis to put an exaggerated emphasis on what he calls craft and sensuality in the character of Dushyanta. He refers to the sad plaints of Hamsapadika,[14] and to the king's admission of 'guilt' in that context to make his point. A simple reference to the epics and other literature in Sanskrit would, however, reveal the error of this emphasis. It was natural for a monarch like Dushyanta to have more than one wife, and the king's 'admission of guilt' is really nothing more than an expression of chivalry of a *rasika*. Not the slightest tinge of moral depravity colours the picture of the king. The voice from the heavens which conveys the glorious purpose of effecting the union of Shakuntala and Dushyanta, and the reactions of sage Kanva, should have set at rest whatever doubt one might have entertained on account of the graphic delineation of amorous passion in the early Acts. Kalidasa seems anxious in that context to ensure that no suggestion of sensuality or licentiousness should tarnish the portrayal. A comparison with the original treatment of the subject in the Mahabharata proves this conclusively.

In Tagore's interpretation of the play one comes across yet other instances of critical exaggeration as, for instance, linking the king's pursuit of the gazelle in the opening scene as a dramatic parallel to his relationship with Shakuntala later. For the present purpose it would suffice to mention that they derive from his basic approach to the play as one built upon a tragi-comic scheme of transgression – chastisement – purification. No doubt, the overt causes of the separation of the lovers are mentioned in the play, and certain limitations of sensibility and vision, which are to be overcome before they may attain the profound facility dramatised in the final Act, are subtly adumbrated. But the design of the play makes it essential that these suggestions do not add up to a moral blemish in the characters. Any over-emphasis on them in European dramatic terms would destroy the moral and emotional balance so carefully contrived by the playwright.

If studies of theme and character along conventional lines of European criticism can mislead, so can rigid formulaic interpretations in terms of Indian poetics. Much of the deficiency in the traditional interpretation of *Abhijnana* has for its origin an incapacity on the part of Sanskrit commentators to rise above standard generalisations of aestheticians. There are, of course, plenty of internal evidence to show that Kalidasa was steeped in the traditional *shastras* and literary works of his time[15], and, therefore, it would be natural to expect in his plays a faithful reflection of contemporary dramatic norms and cultural values. But, then, instances of his indifference to certain conventional prescriptions are also available in his plays.[16] While, therefore, it is clear that his is a sophisticated craft grounded upon the accepted aesthetic tenets of his time, it is equally an independent, original, creative engagement entailing various modifications of the received tradition. Moreover, while emphasising his indebtedness to the *Natyashastra* it is well to remember that, Bharata did not possibly intend all his prescriptions to be binding on a playwright.[17] Sanskrit criticism, however, has generally continued to remain oblivious of such considerations.

The first critical question to be asked in respect of a Sanskrit play is the nature of its final impact, that is, the kind of *sthayi bhava* (basic mental state) it principally stimulates and the *rasa* (aesthetic relish) it engenders. Almost all Indian commentators categorise *Abijnana* as a drama which mainly generates *shringara rasa*[18], making subsidiary use of a host of other aesthetic sentiments like *vatsalya* (the filial), *adbhuta* (the marvellous), *karuna* (the pathetic), *vira* (the heroic), and *santa* (the quiescent), which figure in the play as *vyabhicharins* (subsidiary emotions). They might differ only marginally while discussing the primacy of *sambhoga* (union) or *vipralambha* (separation), but on the basic identification of *shringara* there seems to be almost complete unanimity. The Introduction to the text in the *Haridas Granthamala Series* furnishes a fairly representative account.

> *Abhijnana* is a *nataka* based on the *shringara rasa*. Its *angi rasa* (main aesthetic emotion) is *shringara* and its subsidiary *rasas* are the humorous, the terrible and the filial. A number of subsidiary *bhavas*, too, are experienced in the play. Because of the greater spread in it of *vipralambha shringara*, some hold it to be the main *rasa*. This, however, appears to be incorrect. A *nataka* in Sanskrit does not end in sorrow; it always implies a joyous ending. Moreover Act III

> and VII of *Shakuntala* are built on *sambhoga shringara*. *Vipralambha* naturally precedes (the union) in *nataka* of *shringara rasa*. The *sambhoga* which is found dominant at the conclusion of the drama should be identified as its principle rasa. At the end of Act VII the promise of a permanent union of the hero and the heroine registers the final dramatic impact on the minds of the spectators. Hence, this should be accepted as a *nataka* of *sambhoga shringara*.

On the basis of such criticism, however, it is difficult to explain the nature of the dramatic experience issuing from *Abhijnana*. If the impact of the play in the final scene is to be taken as the most significant pointer, it may be seen that the emotion evoked there through the union of the lovers ranges far beyond the standard associations of *sambhoga shringara*.[19] The meeting in the celestial hermitage symbolises a kind of spiritual advance, and is designed to produce the *santa* with its ultimate emphasis on *moksa* or liberation. The *Bharata vakya* with which the play closes is not simply a conventional prayer. Rightly enough, the theme of this prayer to *Nila Lohita* is liberation from the transient pleasures and pains of mundane life, for such a state of possible bliss and serenity in the characters has been sought to be projected at the end of the play. No doubt, the protagonists are still very much human: the norms of a *nataka* make that obligatory. But they have been carried through various stages of duty, love, suffering and self-purification, and are now presented in a transcendent region, experiencing the three-fold joys of *dharma, artha* and *kama*. These would lead them to the fourth and final attainment, *moksa*, which the playwright can only suggest through poetic-dramatic touches, but cannot really portray in the play.

That *shringara* would not be a proper description of this experience is suggested by a number of critics who discern the working of the *santa rasa* at this stage. Mirashi and Navlekar, for example, draw pointed attention to this:[20]

> In Act VII the predominant sentiment is the quiescent. Its scene is laid in a peaceful, holy atmosphere.... Here the two lovers meet again, but their mutual love is divested of all sensuality by long suffering and by parental kindness... Their aim now is to attain by the path of duty the bliss of final emancipation.

But the finer critical possibilities of this recognition are hardly explored. One usually finds comments such as these being only incidentally dropped in course of a discussion of Act VII. How, if at all, the play has kept this ultimate perspective in focus from Act I itself is generally left unexamined. What is important to discern is not simply the introduction of the 'quiescent' at the final Act, but how the play from its beginnings has modified the love-sequence through different kinds of dramatic emphases so as to logically conclude it with the *santa rasa*. Only on the basis of such a comprehensive structural organisation of another *rasa* can the traditional interpretation of the play as a refined representation of romantic love be pronounced inadequate. If, on the other hand, the *santa* and other *rasas* in it have been only occasionally touched upon, strictly with the objective of illuminating its main erotic content, they would then be viewed as *vyabhichari bhavas*, and the description of the play as one based on *sambhoga shringara* would be unassailable.

Attention may be drawn here to another play by Kalidasa, *Vikramoravshiyam*, which is decidedly built on *sombhoga shringara*. This play has a good many features in common with *Abhijnana*[21]. The main protagonist in either of the plays is an emperor of men and friend to the gods. Each is shown experiencing two phases of *vipralambha*, and achieving a blissful romantic union at the end of each phase. Again, in either case, the love-union is aided and blessed by heavenly powers. Towards the conclusion in both the plays, similarly, the protagonist is presented experiencing thrills of filial joy. In terms of poetic style, too, the plays are similar. But, for all these similarities, they are, in essentials, worlds apart. And the difference does not inhere merely in the structural component, one being a *nataka* and the other a *trotaka*. As S.N. Shastri explains:[22]

> It, therefore, appears that the mixed nature of characters is the only point of difference between a 'Trotaka' and a 'Nataka'; for, in all other respects, the former agrees into with the model of the latter.

And, yet, technically, *trotaka*, is a variety of 'upa-rupaka', a subsidiary form of drama. In any case, Kalidasa thought the space of five Acts in this *trotaka* adequate for purposes of delineating *shringara rasa*, in the purity and intensity of which *Vikramor Vasiyam* has, indeed, few peers. It is, therefore, difficult to see why he intented a broader canvas and a more standard form of *Nataka* in *Abhijnana* to present an identical experience. The explanation, that he might have wished to fashion a more exciting elaboration of the same theme, does not seem very convincing. After all, Kalidasa was one of the most severely economical of artists, and would not need to design an elaborate Seven-Act drama merely to enlarge upon the same *bhava* he has so competently evoked in a shorter space elsewhere. One remembers the song of Hamsapadika floating on to the stage from the background[23]: just a couplet, but a poignant picture of the lady thirsting for the king's love (we never see the lady), in fact, the world she inhabits, is made clear to the audience.

Perhaps the key to the matter is to be discovered in the central Act of the play, which is traditionally accepted as marking the consummation of Kalidasa's dramatic genius. The dominant *rasa* there, strikingly, is *vatsalya* – filial love. An entire Act is prepared to dramatise Shakuntala's parting from her foster-father, from nature which was yet another mother to her, and from the animals to whom she herself had been a foster-mother. Although separation from her friends, too, is movingly delineated, concentration on the filial is preponderant. The question that comes to the mind is, if Kalidasa had planned *vatsalya* to be only a supporting *rasa*, meant to function merely as a *vyabhicharin*, why did he consider it necessary to give it so extended an emphasis and so intense a focus? Another related question that crops up in this context is, whether, as he went along, the dramatist put his main emphasis on a series of mutually-connected *rasas*[24]:

> ...... It (*Abhijanana*) has three predominant sentiments, the erotic (*sringara*) in the first three Acts, the Pathetic (*Karuna*) in next three Acts, and the Quiescent (*santa*) in the last Act. But as the plot develops, it gives rise to occasions for the display of other feelings, which being transient appear and disappear like ripples....

It may, of course, be natural to expect different sentiments attaining prominence at different points in the play, but they have all to be logically connected and directed towards one focal point so that each of these is imbued with some central function. In the absence of such a centripetal ordering of sentiments and emotions there would ensue a dispersal of interest, and the play would exhibit lack of aesthetic cohesion. Coming back, therefore, to the question raised in relation to Act IV, it is necessary to establish its inner connection – apart from the obvious one concerned with the development of story – with both what precedes and what follows in order to examine the appropriateness of the centrality and intensity of *vatsalya*.

In the first three Acts where the erotic is the dominant note it is easy to see that there is something special and unique about its treatment. While on the surface the main concern of the dramatist is to detail out the genesis, growth and consummation of love between Dushyanta and Shakuntala, profounder issues are also being stirred at a deeper level. As an instance we might refer to the tension generated by recounting the history of Shakuntala's birth and her early life. The king discusses the matter at some length with Anasuya and Priyambada, wishing to find out whether the sage intends a life of celibacy for Shakuntala. The answers he receives satisfy him that she is worthy of his attention[25]. But this seemingly casual conversation heightens a sense of dramatic contrast. The anxieties and fears expressed by Shakuntala and her friends in connection with the present romantic development gain an additional intensity in the mind of the audience who are made to remember how she was born of the unholy union of Sage Viswamitra and the heavenly temptress, Menaka, and as a young infant had been *'forsaken'* by her parents. The reference also brings under focus the extraordinary filial attachment reflected in Kanva's tendence of Shakuntala. The apprehension in question would be further deepened by the fact of the *gandharva* form of marriage [26] the lovers contact on their own. One of the functions of Anasuya's question, and the king's answer[27], is to indicate and assuage this tension.

Contrasted to the unholy, temporary union of her parents, Shakuntala's love for Dushyanta is being prepared as an enduring and blissful relationship. This is one reason why Kalidasa takes special pains to emphasis the moral excellence of the two characters. The manifold virtues of Dushyanta, and Shakuntala's tenderness, purity and innocence, are highlighted to indicate the richness of the union to come. As Kanva says, it was a joining together of the noblest of men and the best of woman kind; happily, therefore, he announces – Having united you, the two most accomplished ones, Providence is now blameless for ages[28]. That sensual interest does not constitute the main-spring of their love is repeatedly affirmed by the dramatist, and for all the feeling of infatuation and compulsive love portrayed in the characters in the first three Acts, the nobler dimension of their relationship is never lost sight of.

One might take an extreme example where voluptuous passion is pictured at its most intense, and observe how it gets refined and modified by certain subtle poetic suggestions. In Act II Dushyanta describes the seductive charms of Shakuntala and compares her to 'a flower, the fragrance of which has not yet been enjoyed', 'a tender leaf, which has not yet been disfigured by fingernails', 'a gem, which is still unperforated', and 'an under spoiled fruit of manifold pieties.'[29] As may be seen, Shakuntala is presented first as an object of sensual feast and then viewed as 'the fruits of untarnished piety, a sentiment later iterated by the king in Act VI where he calls her his 'punya-phalam'[30]. From the oblique suggestions of defloration in the 'gem'-image, and of passion in the 'leaf'-image, we come to a more elegant form of sensuality in the 'honey'-image. And all this has been preceded by the tender image of a fragrant flower. Finally, this aesthetic tenderness itself receives a kind of religious transcendence in the image of the fruit of pieties. Against the whole gamut of these suggestions on the nature of Dusyanta's emotion we have the complementary picture of Shakuntala as a graceful blooming creature, a paragon at once of beauty and virtue.

As the playwright delineates gradual rise and growth of passion, he also introduces an extended *vipralambha.* It serves as an instrument both of intensification and test, revealing the true depths of the love of Shakuntala and Dushyanta. It is important to note in this context how it is depicted as intense and consuming, but not as blind passion. As has already been said, the playwright is careful to stress the elements of caution and critical self-examination in both the characters. Shakuntala describes the first stirrings of love in her heart as a '*tapovanavirodhi vikara*'[31] (a sensation contrary to the sentiments proper to a hermitage) and the king compares her to a bright and captivating *suryakanta* gem which can burn the fingers of an unwary wearer. In the present instance, he is in a hermitage, a realm, as he says, of peace and non-violence, but which can be 'a veritable furnace to the sinful'[32]. This fear in the mind of the king (which has nothing really to do with a personal sense of sin) is pictured again and again. In a soliloquy in the beginning of Act III, for instance, he expresses his anxiety that Kanva might misconstrue his love as an act of provocation. He muses:[33]

> I understand the power of tapasya (holy penance and meditation) and also know that Shakuntala is not free to decide things for herself. And, yet, like the stream which cannot move up backwards in its course, my heart refuses to be withdrawn from her (charms).

Clearly, what is portrayed is a deep, obsessive passion, and not blind sensuality.

The first three Acts furnish a variety of evocations besides the erotic. But like Dushyanta at first sight of Shakuntala entranced by the beauty of her '*ratisarbaswam-adhara*', commentators seem to be too obsessed with the erotic to notice other elements the playwright is intently developing. Description of the hermitage, its people and its idyllic environ which are introduced in profusion are interpreted either as appropriate *vibhavas* (setting) for the *erotic*, or as elements contrived to heighten the charms of Shakuntala. It does not seem to be sufficiently appreciated that the playwright is also assiduously suggesting by a variety of means the rich maternal potentiality of Shakuntala. This has been frequently touched upon in Kalidasa-criticism, but does not generally receive the attention it deserves. Of particular importance are the references to the birth of Shakuntala, Kanva's parental solicitude,

Gautami's motherly care, filial affection as expressed by Nature, and most memorably and significantly, Shakuntala's maternal care of the young doe and the plants in the hermitage. The very profusion of such elements suggests that keen evocation of the filial sentiment is of crucial significance to the play. The emphasis on *vatsalya* and the various references to the duties and virtues of life found in the fourth Act suggesting a more refined and higher dimension erotic love ought to attain, have thus been anticipated and prepared for in the first three Acts. The erotic is only a stage in a more comprehensive and sublime amplification leading to a special kind of consummation in filial fulfilment.

In ancient Indian culture marriage was essentially a religiously ordained relationship, serving two sacred purposes – perpetuation of the race and continuity of holy offerings to the manes. A wife was not only one's partner in life from a social point of view, she was also a collaborator in all religious duties and rituals. It was, therefore, natural for Kalidasa to keep the image of '*satputra*' (a worthy offspring) in view while delineating the wooing of a '*satpatni*' (a worthy consort). Cultural values apart, the world of nature itself where the biological drive for mating and an impulse for self-perpetuation seem to be inextricably linked would provide the necessary stimulus to a creative artist to integrate the erotic and the filial. Whatever be the nature of the inspiration, the fact remains that in his poems and plays Kalidasa displays a persistent fascination for themes of procreation and filial passion. And thus we see him in the early Acts of *Abhijnana* already going beyond the initial sentiment of love to what follows, namely, the filial sentiment. Love is not delineated only as a means to personal fulfilment. The higher end to which it is directed would be projected later with the symbolic figure of Sarvadamana at Act VII.

Herein resides the principal difference between *Abhijanana* and *Vikramorvasiyam.* The significance of the child Ayush in the latter play has been overrated. He is peripheral to the main sentiment of the drama.[34] His advent in the stage naturally provides an occasion for Pururava to express filial joy, but *vatsalya* in *Vikramoravasiyam* is used only as a transitory *vyabhicharibhava*, reinforcing Pururava's sense of personal fulfilment at the end of the play. Ironically enough, Ayus is originally fated to bring about a permanent separation between Urvasi and Pururava; the danger is averted only through the intervention of Indra. The main interest of Pururava, and that of the playwright, is focussed all along on the amorous potential of Urvasi. It is interesting to note that, faced with the prospect of separation from her, Pururava thinks of *vanaprastha* (shaking off worldly duties and embracing a life of penance), and not even his duties towards Ayus would hold him back. No higher objective than amorous fulfillment has controlled his plans and actions in the play. In *Abhijanana*, on the other hand, the lovers have been distinctly prepared for nobler attainments. *Vanaprastha*, in their case, would have a more positive spiritual purpose. The incursion of Sarvadamana is central to the plot, and although the audience has a full realisation of it only later, he has been under focus right from the beginning of the play. Intensification of filial sentiment in Act VII is, therefore, experienced as a logical culmination of a process that had been set in motion much earlier.

A number of Indian critics have commented on the extraordinary dramatic power emanating from the figure of Sarvadamana in Act VII, the most notable being Rabindranath. A few European scholars, too, have shown remarkable sensitiveness in responding to this character. Henry W. Wells, for example, makes a profoundly arresting statement.[35] But the subtlety and consistency with which the complex symbolisation of the character has been worked out and projected in the play do not seem to have received adequate attention. The reason seems to lie in the tendency to interpret the play either on the basis of *shringara rasa* or that of romantic allegory which results in a blurring of critical attention in respect of certain significant cues.

Sarvadamana, may it be repeated, is not simply an explicit embodiment of the consummation of the love of Shakuntala and Dushyanta. He has the status of a symbol of the eternal principle of creation and perpetuation of life. For Kalidasa the basis of this principle is the universal impulse of love, an impulse which can be developed as a means to profound self-enrichment as well as social preservation. The first three Acts, in fact, constitute a process to delineate this through Shakuntala. She has gained a marvellous enrichment of personality through her capacious love which embraces the worlds of nature and men. She has known what it is to deeply love, and be loved by, friends and elders, plants and animals, and, finally, by a noble gallant. This process involves a finer and more intense development, namely, the fulfilling experience of filial love. Kalidasa seems to be suggesting that love of such a comprehensive kind and of such intensity as Shakuntala's can be a means to '*tri-varga pratih*'. It is in such a context that her 'tapasya' becomes relevant.[36] *Abhijnana* is designed to prepare a proper background and evoke appropriate sentiments for a love that is at the same time sophisticated and elemental one that conduces equally to worldly and spiritual interests. We have now to follow through the different suggestions with which the theme is elaborated and amplified in the later Acts.

One or two instances may, however, be first cited to show the many subtle forms in which the motif is recurrently, if germinally, introduced in the earlier stretch. Thus at the very beginning of the first Act one encounters an interesting dramatic suggestion. Dushyanta is in pursuit of an antelope. Just as he is about to release his deadly arrow, he hears a loud warning not to kill the animal which belonged to the hermitage. Dushyanta obeys, and a monk who now comes into view expresses his appreciation of this gesture of humility and self-restraint on the part of the king, and offers his blessings:[37]

> This conduct has been worthy of a king born in the race of Puru. May you have a chakravarti (all-conquering) son born to you, endowed with the best of your virtues.

Two other ascetics join and they too, voice the same benediction. The king thereafter advances towards the hermitage. Just as he is about to enter, he experiences a tremor in his right arm, an omen of good fortune, and wonders to himself what 'advancement' for him could possibly lie in store in a hermitage. Significantly enough, he uses the word 'fruit' in this context: an alert audience will naturally connect this 'fruition' with the blessings just offered to the king.

Although Dushyanta cannot anticipate, the hermitage does indeed hold the promise of the fulfillment of the Vaikhanasa's blessings. This suggestion cannot be dismissed as coincidental. For one thing, Kalidasa does not introduce even ordinary elements in his plays in a casual manner, and, secondly, the blessings offered by the monks are not merely a form of conventional greeting. After all, the king's still being issueless must be a matter of concern to all his subjects. And Dushyanta, too, must be experiencing a similar concern on this account. Obviously, therefore, the placing of the blessings, the underpinning by the other two ascetics, and the immediately following omen are deliberately, meaningfully juxtaposed by the playwright. The final Act would make this clearer still.

It may be of some interest to note that the later suffering of both Dushyanta and Shakuntala is presented as issuing from an identical cause-negligence in carrying out parental instructions. Shakuntala fails in the duties of hospitality enjoined upon her by Kanva who was then out on a pilgrimage. Significantly, the pilgrimage had been undertaken by

Kanva in order that certain misfortunes predicted for Shakuntala were averted. As a consequence of her negligence of parental instruction she suffers a curse. Dushyanta, similarly, fails in returning to the palace as enjoined upon him by the queen-mothers where – significantly again – he was being summoned to attend a '*Putrapinda Palana*' ritual.[38] Thus values connected with filial relationship are emphasised in the early Acts in a number of ways.

Act IV which initiates the '*garva sandhi*'[39] is, indeed, the turning point of the drama. Heretofore implicit and indirect suggestions that link the central characters to the filial theme now receive progressively fuller and more direct articulation. With the moving sketches of Shakuntala's parting from nature, from kanva and the other ashramites, from the plants and animals of the hermitage, and other details such as Kanva's concern relating to Priyambada and Anasuya, the numerous filial notes struck through the earlier Acts are carried to a crescendo, as it were. More importantly, from this point onwards the focus begins to turn directly upon the future offspring of the love-union. It is not only casual references, as in parting benedictions like '*vira prasabini bhava*' (may you give birth to a hero) through which the spectator's attention is directed to this important future development. In fact, the entire dramatic design hereafter is conditioned by this vision.

Both Shakuntala and Dushyanta are now treated against two concurrent coordinates of passion, conjugal and filial. In fact, even here in the fourth Act the dramatist is no longer concentrating exclusively on the element of personal affection. The social implications of the love-union of Dushyanta and Shakuntala are already being foregrounded. Thus in the beginning of the Act we are told of a voice from the heavens counselling sage Kanva:[40]

> O Brahman, like the Shami-creeper with its flaming core, your daughter carries the energy of Dushyanta in her womb for the good of the world.

Next we hear about and witness preparations for Shakuntala's departure, and the moving reactions of different persons including those of the sage[41] to the impending separation. This is followed by the famous scene where Kanva and Shakuntala come together for the first time on the stage. The words with which the sage blesses her once again highlight the prospect which the playwright wishes to plant in the spectator's mind:[42]

> My daughter, as Sarmistha was most dear to king Yayati and bore him the future emperor Puru, so, too, may you have your husband's deepest love and

> esteem, and may you be blessed with a child who would be the future emperor.

The verse carriers a number of interesting and complex overtones, but we might only note the reference to Dushyanta as a descendant of the famous emperor Puru, and to the suggestion that the future glory of the race and the stability of the kingdom are associated with the birth of Shakuntala's child.

Towards the end of the scene, again, we find repeated emphases on this aspect, suggesting, as it were, the very reason why the main body of this Act is so heavily saturated with filial sentiment. Thus, when Shakuntala tearfully exclaims that she would find it hard to live away from the hermitage, Kanva says the onerous responsibilities of presiding over the household of Dushyanta would keep her constantly busy, and then adds:[43]

> Just as the Eastern horizon gives birth to the refulgent sun, you would in a few days be the mother of a divine son and would forget the present pangs of separation.

The next verse of Kanva, again, deserves special attention. The final moment of parting has come. A disconsolate Shakuntala begs him to tell her when she might return to the hermitage. Hardly able to master his grief at the moment, the sage is yet keen to emphasise that she was going out with a mission, and should return only after it was fulfilled:[44]

> My daughter, discharge your duties for a long time as the consort of the world's Emperor, produce an indomitable offspring of Dushyanta and (after the child grows mature) investing him with the burdens of government, you may both come to this ashram together to seek liberation.

Clearly, personal love is now being projected as an instrument of general good, and human fulfillment is being envisioned on a vast, comprehensive scale, with transcendence of the self as its climax. Both the lovers would return to the hermitage to go beyond their love.

Act V institutes dramatic reversal. The arguments which are commonly advanced in this context to account for the separation of the lovers have already been referred to. It must here be stressed that in terms of poetic logic, as also common-sense, they are hardly convincing. After all, Shakuntala does not wilfully and deliberately flout her duty. Similarly, in staying behind at the hermitage the king was not really being wilfully disobedient to the queen-mother – it must be realised that what is taken as merely an ostensible reason, namely, protection of the asharamites, is, in fact, an inescapable duty for Dushyanta. Kalidasa has maintained a fine balance, something that Mirashi and Navlekar ignore as they join Rabindranath in advancing the opinion that the manner in which Dushyanta sends away Madhavya to officiate for him at the '*putra pinda palana*' rites proves his craftiness. It has to be appreciated that the playwright has introduced with great discrimination only such elements that serve as a reason for the separation without in any manner causing a blemish on the characters. Only thus can he emphasise the beneficent quality of the 'punishment'. To see in this story of love a transgression of morality is to miss the point entirely. The reversal is meant to enrich – not chastise – the lovers, and to bring into prominence a glorious consummation of their love in the figure of Sarvadamana, or Bharata, whose birth would prove to be a matter of profound gratification to the world at large.

Before we leave this Act, we should note three important references with a memorable bearing on the element of *vatsalya.* First, while reminding Dushyanta of their past relationship, Shakuntala alludes to an incident[45] involving an interesting confrontation between the two kinds of love which at the moment are under equal emphasis. With Shakuntala at the centre, the erotic and the filial had then been brought together, and the young doe featuring in the incident was meant to serve as a significant emblem in the context of the play's thematic pattern. Secondly, as has been rightly emphasized by Ratnamayidevi Dikshit,[46] in the exchange between the king and Shakuntala the latter feels provoked beyond endurance only when Dushyanta makes a fling at her motherhood by referring to the wiles of a certain mother-bird.[47] Thirdly, as the disconsolate and helpless Shakuntala is being led out by the priest, it is her heavenly mother who comes to her rescue, emphasizing at this point the element of parental solicitude and care. [48] Each of these references poignantly reinforces the filial sentiment.

Act VI, to start with, seems to be concentrating exclusively on a conventional representation of *vipralambha.* But the grief of separation is only an aspect of Dushyanta's sorrow. There are three marked stages through which his grief is expounded and amplified – the mourning of the gallant in isolation is aggravated by the remorse of a conscience-stricken, virtuous soul, and further deepened through the distress of a lover brooding over the suffering of his beloved. But there are yet more agonising dimensions to his misery which he comes to properly recognise when called upon to settle the issue of inheritance after a rich merchant in the kingdom dies intestate. Rejection of Shakuntala, he now realises, has forced his ancestors, too, into a state of deep despair, for there would be no one after him to offer them their due oblations.[49] By implication, he himself faces a similar prospect in his after-life. The loss of Shakuntala might thus mean a terrible misfortune – extinction of the great dynasty of the Purus.[50] Shakuntala, in terms of the Hindu theology, was the means of alleviating his *tritapa*-material, metaphysical, and spiritual sufferings. Only now does he recognise the full significance of her love, and understands how she stood for 'all that is auspicious in life' ('shreyas'). But the realisation, he believes, has come too late – instead of being a source of bliss and deliverance, now it only serves to aggravate his feelings of loss and despair.

Even during the period of his early infatuation, we now remember, his attention was not confined to Shakuntala's youthful charms. As he asserted before the girls in Act II, she embodied a far greater promise:[51]

> I may have many other wives. But there are only two seats on which the glories of my race would be erected-one, the ocean – girdled earth, and the other, your friend here.

Something we might then have thought was only a form of courtly adulation, was, indeed, an earnest statement of faith. As has been earlier discussed, grand possibilities envisioned through Shakuntala were being carefully unravelled before the spectator from the beginning. Now, at the end of Act VI it is Dushyanta who is having a fuller and clearer recognition of her significance. Not the amorous, but the maternal potential of Shakuntala now takes hold of his mind. He goes on to compare his fate to that of 'a person who has already sown on his fertile land seeds of his future sustenance and security, but who, in a moment of stupidity, sells it away'. The 'religiously sanctioned union' with Shakuntala had helped 'the seeds of glory and of stability of his race to germinate, but in his ignorance, he had rejected that source of future blessedness'[52]. Like the holy waters of the Saraswati, Shakuntala was to have sanctified his race, but his sinfulness, he says, has dried up that stream of salvation.[53] The focus of dramatic interest has clearly shifted from the *person* of Shakuntala to the *promise* she held – from the beloved to the '*dharma patni*' who would bring forth a '*satputra*'

At the end of Act VI, therefore, we see how the king's vision of love (and Shakuntala's, as well, as we learn from the asides of Sanumati)[54] has attained a new maturity. It is only proper that the reunion should now take place in an appropriate manner. And so the gods contrive their union in the blessed abode of Hemakuta. It is a mellowed Dushyanta, fresh from an exhilarating and glorious battle in defence of the divinely appointed order, who is conducted to the celestial hermitage. It is important to note that the king has been spiritually reinvigorated before the meeting takes place. 'Both in the inner world and the outer environment I now experience a certain quietude', he says. Dushyanta, that is to say, had to grow in knowledge and vision, and attain to a higher refinement of being, before he could qualify for the supreme felicity symbolied by the union with Shakuntala.

In course of their descent from the heaven the king draws the attention of Matali to a refulgent range of mountains and is told it was Hemakuta, the hermitage of Kashyapa (Maricha) and Aditi, parents of the gods. Unknown to the king, Shakuntala had embraced a life of austerity and penance there. And it is there that the reunion is to be solemnised in the presence of the primal parents. The holy significance of enacting the reunion under the auspices of the first parents of the world is, of course, obvious. More specifically, by introducing Kashyapa and Aditi, whose children rule the heavens while they remain engaged in penance, and who symbolise the noblest ideals of conjugal harmony and bliss, Kalidasa indicates the kind of fulfillment Dushyanta and Shakuntala are to seek on earth. Such an aspiration, we now remember, had been counselled by Kanva in his parting words to Shakuntala. As Kalidasa had earlier emphasised in the epic *Kumarasambhavam*, 'a worthy wife is one's main support in religious pieties'[55]. Dushyanta and Shakuntala have to return to their earthly duties and earn 'purusartha' (merit), for that is their dharma'. It is for the same religious merit that they should seek 'artha' (material prosperities) and it is to the same end that their 'Kama' (desire) has to be directed. A symbol of all these felicities would now be presented in the form of their child, Sarvadamana, the all subduing

As they approach the hermitage, Matali points at an oleander plant which stood near the cottage of the divine couple. His comment is interesting: 'The divine mother Aditi has carefully watered and tended this plant'. Through poetic suggestion this causes an immediate flash-back – Dushyanta having his first sight of Shakuntala while she was watering the plants in Kanva's hermitage. This also suggests the main reason for Shakuntala being assigned the duty of tending the plants and other creatures: it was intended to serve as a training in maternal sensibility. The oleander plant embodies the maternal instinct of Aditi which embraces all living things, and the playwright had a purpose in making Matali pointedly refer to the plant, and offer an explanation of its presence there. Critical justification for this reading can also be derived from a similar context in Kalidasa's *Raghubamsam* where Valmiki enjoins upon Sita the task of watering the plants in the ashram:[56]

> with pitchers filled with water which you are able to carry, you would water the plants of the hermitage. Thereby, you will surely experience the love of a child even before your own child is born.

After the brief exchange with Matali, the king moves into the premises of the hermitage. As he does so, he experiences a tremor in his right arms – something, we recall, the playwright had inscribed once before at the beginning of the play when Dushyanta was entering the hermitage of Kanva. We remember, too, the emphasis in the blessings then offered by the monks. After long years Dushyanta is going to experience, dramatically, the 'fruition' of the good omen. To start with, however, it has an initial effect of making him morose, and he exclaims:[57]

> I keep no hopes of getting what I long for; O arms, why do you vibrate for nothing? I have in the past scorned the one good of my life and, in consequence, now I will suffer miseries only.

The real significance of the tremor in his arms, as discussed earlier, should no more be in doubt.

The child Sarvadamana is now revealed. He is seen forcing apart the jaws of a lion-cub to count its teeth, while two women attendants vainly attempt to release the cub from his iron grip. The king stands gazing at him, marvelling at his strength and courage, and feels strangely drawn towards him. He moves closer, and discovers on the plams of the child all the marks of a 'chakravarti', something that had featured in the blessing of the Vaikhanasa, and had been later adduced by the royal priest in Act V as a future token to establish Shakuntala's true relationship with the king. Dushyanta expresses his envy at the good fortune of the child's parents and poignantly pours forth his yearning and deep wistfulness. He encapsulates the joys of parenthood in four supremely evovative lines[58] which in terms of their simple realism and emotional exhilaration are said to be unsurpassed in world literature. This, the play underscores, is the kind of fulfillment *shringara* leads to at the level of common mankind. At a higher level, there are still other, nobler possibilities.

The identity of Sarvasamana is now revealed to the king in a gradual, dramatic manner. The attendants of the child, noting with surprise a certain magical sign which goes to show that it is the child's father who now stands by him, run out to inform Shakuntala who is 'engaged in penance' ('*niyama – vyaritayah*'). In a rush of joy the king presses Sarvadamana to his heart, and intones to himself, 'Why should I not greet the *fulfilment of all my wish*'. The emphasis in the last clause deserves particular attention. Sarvadamana embodies the fulfillment of the love of Dushyanta and Shakuntala – and much more besides, as the play would make clear. Shakuntala now comes in dressed as an ascetic, and the lovers stand facing each other. Each finds the other grown wan and emaciated through protracted suffering. Deep regret and bliss of reunion fear lest the past should repeat itself, and hope of a glorious future – a complex body of feelings and emotions – now agitate their hearts, and it is only with difficulty that they can properly express themselves. An important point that is brought home at this stage relates to the element of humility now discerned in the lovers. Both had revealed strains of arrogant self-righteousness during their last meeting (Act V). Now is witnessed a complete change. Dushyanta's prayer for the forgiveness'-abject, one would say, if one failed to grasp its conventional quality and the inner change already wrought in him – and Shakuntala's comment, that perhaps some sin from their past life had caused a temporary barrier to rise between them, reveal the understanding and humility both have gained in course of their suffering. The scene highlights qualities that are essential for one's growth in virtue and spirituality.

Even as the playwright projects the reunion at a higher visionary plane, he is also keen to portray ordinary, human reactions of the couple.[59] Only an illustrative phrase may be picked up from the context to show the pithy delineation. When Sarvadamana enquires about the identity of the stranger, his mother can only mutter in a voice choking with emotion: *bhagayedhani prichcha* (Ask your fate). It is a dramatically multivalent phrase suggesting, first, that *human* identification had not been adequate on the earlier occasion to establish Shakuntala's identity, and secondly, that the future of Sarvadamana depended on the recognition of his legitimacy by the king. The words convey a sense of apprehension that still lingers in her mind, revealing traces of a sad fatalism. More than all these, however, it constitutes a spontaneous, emotionally charged expression of deep sorrow and *abhimana*. Ever since she has come into his presence, she has been fighting her emotions from coming to the surface, and the broken voice brings out how the innocent enquiry of Sarvadamana results in a sudden upsurge, threatening to tear apart her precarious restraint.

At the same time as personal emotions are thus intimately portrayed, the broader significance of the union is not ignored. The two major aspects – personal and general – are both directly highlighted and subtly evoked through poetic suggestions. The king, for example, compares their meeting with the union of Chandrama (moon-god) and Rohini, the dearest of His consorts, after a period of eclipse.[60] The eclipse, for the moon-god, constituted a 'personal' tragedy and in those days a matter of universal concern. The period of eclipse is considered, even today, inauspicious; it symbolises a temporary victory of evil over good. Thus, with the personal bliss of Chandrama's reunion with Rohini there is also associated a sense of deliverance for the world. The darkness covering the face of the earth is lifted, and the time becomes wholesome and auspicious again. The union of Dushyanta and Shakuntala is suggested to be a similarly auspicious and blessed event, both for the lovers and for the world at large.

The words of Matali, who now returns to the stage and felicitates Dushyanta, contain a significant indication of the direction of dramatic interest:

> O king, you have now achieved real prosperity through the good fortune of your union with the religiously wedded wife and the sight of the face of your son.

He informs the king that Maharshi Kashyapa (Maricha) would now give them audience. The royal family, therefore, move forward to sanctify their good fortune – *abhyudaya kala*, as Dushyanta puts it – in the sacred presence of the mythic couple. Dushyanta's desire to present himself with Shakuntala holding Sarvadamana in front of her is of particular significance. His words – *Shakuntale, Avalambyatam putra* – pointedly draw attention to the foregrounding of Sarvadamana here. Interesting, again, is the way Maricha introduces Dushyanta to Aditi, saying he was the one who led the wars of 'your son, Indra'.

The filial note is once again sounded in the words of Matali who draws attention to *'putra priti pisunena chakshusa'* (eyes reflecting filial love) with which the divine parents look at the family of Dushyanta. Both Maricha and Aditi address Dushyanta and Shakuntala as son and daughter respectively. Strikingly, again, Shakuntala touches their feet declaring. 'I offer worship at thine feet with my son'. Aditi's benediction and greeting specially point at the significance of Sarvadamana – he is, she says, the symbol of prosperity and blessedness for the lineage of both his parents. And, then, the various emphases on the focal point, both direct and indirect, which we have observed through the play receive one of their clearest articulations in Maricha's words to the king:

> It is through good fortune that you have been united with the pure and dedicated Shakuntala and with your worthy child. Seeing you together it looks as if there has been a union of Faith, Fortune and Virtuous Performance.

The king's answer, again, highlights the 'fruit' of his '*sampada*' – Sarvadamana stands as a symbol of that prosperity and fruition. Only here in the final Act does one properly realise how this has all along been the objective before the play. It is with such a noble synthesis and not *shringara* in conventional terms, that the play has been seized from the very beginning.

The centrality of Sarvadamana in such a scheme would once again be affirmed, to strike as it were, the concluding note of the play. But, before that is done, it is necessary to remove whatever traces of discomfort and doubt might have lingered in the minds of Dushyanta and Shakuntala. Accordingly, Maricha explains to them the manner in which the curse of Durbasa had caused a temporary amnesia in Dushyanta and brought about their separation. The message of the reunion is then sent out to 'father' Kanva. Maricha now turns to Dushyanta and asks him whether he had already greeted his son; Sarvadamana, after all, is the most authentic embodiment and guarantee of the fullness and fulfilment of their love. Finally, as if to underscore at the end of the play the magnificence implicit in the symbol of the child, Kashyapa prophesies a glorious future awaiting him.[61]

> This child of yours would inspire awe all around, conquering all the seven continents and carrying his banner to the shores of the high seas without causing harm to anyone. He had subdued all animals in the hermitage and hence was popularly known here as 'Sarvadamana'. In future he would be fulfilling the needs of the whole world and would, therefore, be known as the caretaker of the world.

Thus, in conclusion, Kalidasa is not merely striking the final *santa* chords in a sequence of *sambhoga shringara*, as has been the traditional view, but more significantly, also heightening the entire dramatic event through the mythic symbol of the Primal Parents and concretising the consummation of love in the symbol of Sarvadamana. Since as a playwright he is concerned with suggesting potentialities for fourfold fulfillment in the human condition, he has had to develop a human object and situation to carry this symbolic burden. Embodying the profound love of Dushyanta and Shakuntala, connecting the past with the present, the human world with the non-human, and the domestic and personal with the social and transcendental, Sarvadamana is made to evoke such a supreme attainment. The personal salvation (only secondarily, social welfare) sought by king Dilipa and queen Sudakshina (as also a few other royal couples) in *Raghubamsam*, and the universal salvation sought through the consummation of love between Lord Shiva and Uma in *Kumarasambhabam,* are fused and delicately humanised in the career of Shakuntala and Dushyanata. Clearly, Goethe's famous comments on the play are not an outburst of undiscriminating adulation; *Abhijnana* does, indeed, offer such a rich fare.

Two of the main points which emerge out of the present discussion, namely, stress on the fourth and final *purusartha* of *moksa* and the major importance assigned to *vatsalya* do not receive emphasis in the *Natyashastra.* Bharata does not mention *vatsalya* as a major *rasa*[62], and he seems to suggest that, *moksa* being implicit in the generic term *dharma*, it does not form a separate objective to be specially explored by the dramatist.[63] And the *Natyashastra* is the only one among authoritative and systematic works of dramatics known to us which serves as a frame of reference for Kalidasa's plays. As a great creative artist, while conforming to as many of Bharata's prescriptions as possible, Kalidasa is also guided by his own insight and vision of things. A critical procedure which refuses to respect both his obligation and freedom would, therefore, fail to do justice to the immense scope of *Abhijnana.*

Notes and Refernces

References to the text are from *Abhijnana Shakuntalam*, Haridas Sanskrit Series, Seventh Edition. (The Chowkhamba Sanskrit Studies Series, Varanasi, 1972) – hereafter referred simply as *Abhijnana.*

1. For example, K.C. Pandey, *Comparative Aesthetics*, Vol. I, The Chowkhamba Sanskrit Studies Series, Varanasi, 1959.
2. See, J.Gassner, *Masters of the World Drama*, Dover Edition, 1954, pp. 116-120. Similarly, A.A.Macdonell asserts: "While Kalidasa stands highest in poetical refinement, in tenderness and depth of feeling the author of the *Mrichchakatika* is pre-eminent among Indian playwrights for the distinctively dramatic qualities of vigour, life and action, no less than sharpness of characterization, being thus allied in genius to Shakespeare". A.A.Macdonell, *A History of Sanskrit Literature*, Munshiram Manoharlal Publications, 1961, p. 364.
3. "Melodrama", not in any pejorative sense; it is meant to suggest that concentration on psycho-pathologically more compelling emotions such as terror, and emphasis on the overtly theatrical and the declamatory to heighten the dramatic impact, are not considered desirable in the context of the form of *Nataka* to which *Abhijnana* belongs.
4. "Tragedy is clean, it is restful, it is flawless. It has nothing to do with melodrama. Tragedy is restful, and the reason is that hope, that foul deceitful thing, has no part in it." *Antigone*, Jean Anouilh, Methuen & Co. Ltd., (Paperback)1969, p. 34-5.
5. Cyrus Hoy, *The Hyacinth Room*, Chatto & Wyndus, London, 1964.
6. Plays are divided into ten main types (therefore, *Dasa Rupaka*) out of which only half are considered to be of a sufficiently delicate and refined order – *Sukumara.*

Nataka is the highest type of drama in the Indian tradition. For details, see, B.Shukla (ed.), *Natakalaksanaratnakosa*, Chawkhamba Sanskrit Series Office, Varanasi, 1972, pp. 3-14.

7. *Vaidarbhiriti* is a tender and gay lyrical mode. This is appropriate for characters with delightful vivacity of conduct and bearing – *Kaisiki Vritti.* See, Natya Sastra Ch. XVIII.

8. SJ.Robert Antoine, *Greek Tragedy and Sanskrit Drama*, Jadavpur Journal of Comparative Literature, Vol. 8, p. 45.

9. V.V.Mirashi & N.R. Navlekar, *Kalidasa*, Popular Prakashan, Bombay, 1969, p. 357.

10. *Natya Sastra*, Ch. XVII.

11. Ratnamayidevi Dikshit, ("The curse of Durbasa came as a chastisement"), *Women in Sanskrit Drama*, Delhi, p. 154.

12. *"Na ca pariharya vastuni Dushyantasya manah pravarttate"* – II. 8(-). Also, earlier, *"Asamsayam ksatraparigraha ksama yadarthamasyamabhilasi me manah/Satam hi sandehapadesu vastusu Pramanamantahkaranaprabrittayah"* (I. 21). The hero of a *Nataka*, incidentally, was expected to be a *Rajarshi* in accordance with Bharata's prescriptions.

13. *Abhijnana*, II. 15.

14. Ibid. V. 8.

15. In the introduction to his edition of *Abhijnana*, Surendradev Sastri (as corrected by C Tripathy, Ramnarayan Venimadhab, 1977, p. 53-56), offers a list of the wide-ranging references available in *Abhijnana* alone. Also, see, Kapildev Dwivedi, *Abhijnana Shakuntalam*, Sahitya Sansthan, Allahabad, 1978, pp. 46-9.

16. R.S. Tiwari, *Mahakavi Kalidasa*, Vidyabhavan Rashtrabhasa Granthamala, 1961, pp. 323-4. Provides a catalogue of Kalidasa's departures from the *Natya Sastra.*

17. "Bharata does not lay down any hard and fast rules which have to be blindly followed" K.C.Pandey, op. cit., p. 391.

18. Cf. Dwivedi and Sastri, op. cit., Some like Dr. Jamuna Pathak do not even discuss it, presumably because, to them it is a settled, well-known matter. See, J. Pathak (ed.), *Abhijnana Shakuntalam*, Mudiyar, Gajipur, 1978. Also, see, *Abhijnana Shakuntalam,* University Publication, Varanasi, 1977. Dr. Surendradev Sastri calls it (op. cit., p. 108) *Karuna- Vipralambha Shringara*, and finds at Act IV *Vatsalya-Vipralambha Shringara.* How he brings in Shringara here is somewhat mystifying. Dwivedi (op. cit., p. 63) calls it simply *Vatsalya-Vipralambha*, and sees in the later Act *Karuna-Vipralambha.*

19. There have been later aestheticians who consider *Shringara* as the only *rasa* as, for example, Bhoja in *Shringara Prakaasa.* Abhinavagupta also emphasized that 'rasa' is one and indivisible, and that it needs no adjective. But these are an all-inclusive use of aesthetic terms for purposes of defining the ultimate or transcendental state of aesthetic experience. Once these critics come to the question of defining distinct kinds of experience in particular plays they, too, narrow down the import

of the term 'Sringara'. Thus Bhoja admits twelve *rasas* in his *Saraswati Kanthabharana*. Similarly, Bharata offers, first of all, a broad implication of 'Shringara' to suggest "all that. is „ pure, beautiful and sacred, on earth" (*Yatkmchilloke Shuchimedhyamujjvalam darshaniyam va tatshringarenopamiyate*). But further discussions in his *Natya Sastra* lead to the specific form – "Its media are worthy young men and women: it has two forms, *Sambhoga* and *Vipralambha*" (*Sa ca stree-purusahetuka uttamoyubaprakritih. Tasya dve adhisthane. Sambhoga Vipralambha-scha*). Shringara here means the aesthetic experience of love between a man and a woman. It has no implications of gross sensuality, though it emphasizes the amorous and the erotic in a refined form.

20. *Kalidasa*, op. cit., p. 313.
21. For a discussion on the similarities, see, R.S. Tiwari, op. cit., pp. 315-8.
22. S.N. Shastri, *The Laws and Practice of Sanskrit Drama*, The Chowkhamba Sanskrit Studies Series, Vol. XIV, 1961, p. 27.
23. *Abhijnana*, V. 8.
24. V.V.Mirashi and N.R.Navlekar, op. cit., p. 311.
25. Unlike a flirtsome Casanova which some have made him out to be, clearly the king acts with a mature sense of responsibility in eliciting all information regarding Shakuntala before committing his emotions.
26. A.C.Burnell, Cf. *The Ordinances of Manu,* Trans., Oriental Books Reprint Corpn., Second Edition, 1971, pp. 47-8. While this explains Kanva's fears and the comments of Gautami and Sargarava in Act V, it must also be remembered that for the ruling classes this form of marriage was not considered disreputable. Instances in the epics and Puranas are legion. Also, note Dushyanta's argument – III.28.
27. *Abhijnana*, III. 23.
28. Ibid., V. 16.
29. Ibid., II. 11.
30. Ibid., VI. 10.
31. Ibid., I.27 (-).
32. Ibid., II. 7.
33. Ibid., III. 2.
34. Aurobindo's reading of the significance of Ayus is an overstatement: "And their child is Ayus, human life and action glorified and ennobled by contact with the divine. It is, therefore, one of the most profound and splendid of the many profound and splendid allegories in the great repertory of Hindu myth that Kalidasa has here rendered into so sweet, so natural, and passionate a story of human love and desire. The same extraordinary vividness of feeling and imagination is poured over Ayus when Pururava finds himself a father; never had the passion of paternity been expressed with such vivid concreteness or with such ardent sensuousness of feeling" – Sri Aurobindo Birth Centenary Library, Deluxe Edition, Vol. 3, p. 271. Such a symbolic power of Ayus is not borne out by the

text. The filial sentiments of Pururavas have, of course, been movingly painted, but the words of Aurobindo would be more appropriate with reference to Sarvadamana in *Abhijnana.*

35. "Like Dante's great poem, both Blake's work and that of the Indian playwright carry us on the rotating wheels; all art stops where the ultimate or mystic vision begins. The still point about which the wheel turns may be described only as motionless and silent. But drama and poetry are primarily concerned with imagined things, seen and heard. They are of the world of art and to both Blake and the Sanskrit playwright art, symbolised either as Blake's Los or Kalidasa's Bharata, represents the highest imaginative fruition" – H.W.Wells (ed.), *Six Sanskrit Plays*, Asia Publishing House, New York, 1964, General Introduction, P. XXII; "Both his two masterpieces are myths for the stage and must be so understood and presented if they are to yield their true meaning. The heroine, Shakuntala, in other words, must not be made to resemble Goethe's Dorothea,... Her play is not a romantic drama but a Sacred drama". *The Classical Drama of India*, Asia Publishing House, 1963, p. 27.

36. Tagore develops an elaborate comparison between the tapasya of Uma and that of Shakuntala. It should be noted that Kalidasa does not emphasize this aspect overmuch. For all their similarities, the fundamental difference between Uma and Shakuntala must never be lost sight of. *Abhijnana*, being a *nataka*, renders it in more directly *human* terms. Tagore's interpretation of a powerfully human sentiment in Shakuntala's answer to Bharata – 'Bhagayedhani Prucha' (Ask your fate) becomes falsified by the over-emphasis on Shakuntala's '*tapasya'*.

    Cf. S.N. Dasgupta's comment :

    "Strictly speaking, there was no *tapasya* for love (In *Abhijnana Shakuntalam*);.... We cannot also apply the norm of *Kumara Sambhavam* to the drama *Shakuntala*.... We cannot also hold that Kalidasa believed that suffering through separation chastens love,".... S.N.Dasgupta and S.K.De, *A History of Sanskrit Literature*, Vol. I, University of Calcutta, 1977, p. xxxvii.

37. *Abhijnana*, 1.12

38. The ritual was meant to ensure 'pinda' (ritual offerings) for one's after-life in case the death of one's son preceded one's own. The importance of the observances by a son for the peace of his parents' after-life is emphasized.

39. Sanskrit theorists discussed five connecting points in the development of the plot –

"Mukha Sandhi", "Pratimukha Sandhi", "Garva Sandhi", "Avamarsha Sandhi", and "Nirvahana Sandhi". 'Sandhi' means the link and 'Garva' means concealed (the womb). This is the middle link in the plot.

40. *Abhijnana*, IV. 6.

41. Ibid., IV. 8.

42. Ibid., IV. 9.

43. Ibid., IV. 21.

44. Ibid., IV. 22.
45. Ibid., IV. 22 (-).
46. "The wife's patience gives way to the indignation of the mother". Ratnamayi Devi Dikshit, op. cit., p. 93.
47. *Abhijnana*, V. 23.
48. Ibid., V. 33.
49. Ibid., VI. 27.
50. Ibid., VI. 28.
51. Ibid., III. 23.
52. Ibid., VI. 26.
53. Ibid., VI. 27.
54. Ibid., VII. 9.
55. *Kumara Sambhavam*, VI. 13.
56. *Raghubamsam*, XIV. 78.
57. *Abhijnana*, VII. 13.
58. Ibid., VII. 17.
59. Ibid., VII. 23 & 24 (-).
60. Ibid., VII. 22.
61. Ibid., VII. 33.
62. For the history of the development of *Vatsalya* as a category of *rasa*, see, V.Raghavan, *The Number of Rasas*, Adyar, Madras, 1975,pp. 119-125.
63. Authors of *Natya Darpana, Mandara-Maranda*, and *Rasarnava Sudhakara* separately mention this fourth 'purushartha' as an objective of dramatic 'rasa'. See, S.N.Shastri, op. cit., p. 11.

CHAPTER 3

Mrichchakatikam: Thematic and Tonal Patterns

With more than thirty characters to enact the *prakarana* through ten elaborate Acts, making use of seven varieties of Prakrit in addition to chaste Sanskrit, harnessing almost all the major *rasas*, and pressing into service a wide-ranging social life spanning the plebeian and the aristocratic, Shudraka's *Mrichchakatikam* achieves dramatic synthesis on a large, inclusive scale. For all its vastness of design, however, there is no sign of structural looseness or diffuseness of dramatic appeal. Selecting an unconventional story of passion and love for its main subject, and inscribing a broader public event of political upheaval into the subsidiary plot, the playwright explores possibilities of integration in respect of various dualities and dichotomies which disturb and dislocate human life at the individual and social levels. The play, therefore, registers the impact of both a great work of art and an incisive social document.

More than its large social appeal and the exciting bustle and sweep of theatrical performance, however, the subtle working out of thematic and emotional antinomies in the play should constitute its major interest for us today. Dramatic interest generated by the interaction of characters and development of plot is intensified and expanded here by the submarine engagement of a fleet of thematic 'tensions'. But, as is well-known, Indian critics of the play have, for the most part, concentrated on emotional designing of *rasa* and have neglected the critical area of theme-study. Western critics, on other hand, not suspecting the presence of thematic complexity in Sanskrit plays, have mostly remained content by emphasising the play's realistic appeal. Unlike in the case of many other Sanskrit plays, however, critical concern for thematic structures is of fundamental importance here.[1]

Like all great tragi-comedies, *Mrichchakatikam* engages itself in thematic exploration in two main directions: it seeks to discover values which help sustain a harmonious social order, and to delineate qualities of mind and heart necessary for achieving fulfillment at individual, inter-personal and social levels. It is at once serious and carefree, treating the comic and tragic potentialities of social life together in order to illumine some higher means to individual fulfillment. As different from tragedy, social context is constantly kept in view here, and its thematic structures have more of a social than a metaphysical orientation.[2] Similarly, an emphasis on deeper levels of individual being while envisioning possibilities of human fulfillment keep it apart from traditional comedies. Personal value and social conduct are studied together as means to the establishment of a superior order of harmony and joy. A profound dramatic interest is at work in Shudraka's choice of a multitude of characters – 'all in the round', as Warder emphasizes[3], encompassing a wide spectrum of social life. The play thus presents a significant ordering of human material, comprehending a variety of motifs and themes.

One might, for instance, note the opposition between art and trade which is introduced at many points in the play. On a superficial observation this may appear to be a casual strain, but it constitutes one of the fundamental socio-personal themes under examination. Dealing as it does with the sophisticated, metropolitan life in the capital city of Ujjayini, *Mrichchakatikam* attempts a study of the tension generated by values and obligations involving two alternative approaches to vocation – mercenary and aesthetic. It projects the necessity of transforming one's profession into an elevating, artistic experience and thereby deriving a feeling of fulfilment out of inter-personal relationship. A number of secondary characters in the play enact the experiences of people who seek to bring to their vocations the discrimination and relish of artistic connoisseurs. However ordinary-nay, even debased-be their occupation, the characters display a singular urge to discover therein possibilities of higher refinement and aesthetic gratification. The self-conscious and deliberate manner in which many of them engage in 'trade as art' forces one to reexamine certain of the things which are ordinarily glossed over as incidental, casual matter; and the clear pattern which then emerges, involving the central protagonists as also the secondary characters, convinces one of a conscious dramatic design at work. Obviously, this has particular relevance for the social segment comprising artisans and tradesmen in populous cities. Shudraka's concentration on this theme illuminates one aspect of his *civilised* art.

Even as ordinary a character as Samvahaka, the masseur, is keenly alive to the tension between values of art and trade. As he emphasises in course of his talk with Vasantasena in Act II, he used to derive a deep measure of satisfaction while cultivating his delicate art in the service of the noble Charudatta. The rich aesthetic and moral sensibility of Charudatta, Samvahaka suggests, helped to transform the lives of his attendants. With Charudatta's fortune in decline, he rues, he no longer has the scope to practise it with elegance and sophistication. That his discontent is a consequence of his present inability to derive any artistic satisfaction from his work is made absolutely clear:[4]

> Vasantasena – It is a very delicate art that you have learnt !
>
> Samvahaka – Lady, it is true I learnt it as an art, but now it is only a means to my livelihood.

Lest the audience should miss the point, the playwright further introduces a pointed comment by an attendant of Vasantasena's – 'you have given a reply indicative of extreme dejection' – to underscore the burden of sadness in Samvahaka's voice. Forced to practise his art at a pedestrian level, as merely a trade that brings him his physical upkeep, he suffers acute psychological depression and goes to the gaming table in search of relief.

A similar urge for aesthetic satisfaction is dramatised even in as uncongenial a situation as house-breaking. Shudraka is not bothered by the attendant danger of appearing artificial and fastidious as he presents Sarvilaka soliloquising on the scientific skill and artistic elegance he wished to display in digging a passage through the wall of Charudatta's house. It is remarkable that Sarvilaka is allowed to adopt an almost poetic attitude in such an inapposite context. A note of artistic delight is unmistakeable in his words:[5]

> Should I dig the hole in the shape of a full-blown lotus or a half-moon, or a spacious pond, a triangle or a swastik or a full pitcher? Where and how should I demonstrate my art so that the townsfolk tomorrow would be wonderstruck by looking at it?

Later Charudatta is presented observing the breach and admiring the beauty and precision of the digging. His words on that occasion not only reveal his sensitiveness to beauty at all times, but also vindicate the uncommon skill and artistic temperament of the burglar.

It may be noted here that Sarvilaka is not just an ordinary thief. He is, no doubt, adept at house-breaking, but he looks upon his skill as an artistic accomplishment and a thrilling game and not a means of livelihood. His aspiration and taste are of a higher order. His present exploit, for instance, is a desperate venture to acquire ransom to liberate the girl he loves from her bonded state. Even so, he expresses revulsion against the deed. The later scenes bring to the fore an altogether different dimension of his character – his capacity for noble, unselfish action. As he is on his way to consummate his union with his beloved, he comes to know that his 'friend' Aryaka was being persecuted by the king and was in desperate straits. At once he resolves to do his duty, and turning his back upon the felicity he had been so assiduously pursuing, rushes to the aid of the political rebel. A similar sensitiveness and capacity for lofty actions distinguishes Samvahaka, too. The passion with which he reacts to life's chequered shade, and turns his back upon worldly allurements to join an order of monks, shows only the reverse side of a coin whose obverse face had been presented in the beginning in his singular observations on the quality of his trade.

Both Sarvilaka and Samvahaka dramatise the subjugation of artistic taste by commonplace – even abject – states of life, and ways of enriching individual and social existence. Equally they convey the message that unless the professional self receives a heightening touch and acquires an aesthetic dimension, it may ultimately lead to emotional atrophy and moral debasement. Enrichment of life through the adoption of an artistically and morally elevating perspective, and degeneration of life in the absence of it – this may, in fact, be one way of summing up the entire subject-matter of the play. Shudraka dramatises the interaction between values of trade and art in such an inclusive thematic context.

Thus we find a remarkable interplay between a professional wooer and a sensitive connoisseure, between the mind of an artful pander and that of an artist, in the character of the Vita. As a love-companion to Shakara, the king's brother-in-law, he is first of all seen performing his duty of wooing the reluctant courtesan, Vasantasena, with wonderful wit and felicity. The sensitiveness and refinement reflected in his speech clearly indicate an essentially poetic disposition.[6] Very soon we notice how his artistic temperament (a qualification that is prescribed by tradition for such a character) makes him despise certain actions he is called upon to perform as a professional wooer. Being in the employ of an uncouth, lustful character is a matter of profound dissatisfaction to him. While he performs his duty of furthering Shakara's amorous interests, displaying superb elegance and lyrical verve, he also experiences deep psychological discomfort over this aesthetically and morally repellent task of aiding brutish lust. Thus, in course of his very first appearance itself, while he reels off a series of brilliant poetic arguments, enticing Vasantasena to his master, he also expresses his disgust at Shakara's boorishness in a number of brief asides.

Once again, we have here a case similar to Samavahaka's 'trade minus art'. When it caters to physical passion, his service declines into a trade; but, in the context of the higher romantic love, it grows into an exquisite instrument of aesthetic gratification. It is the artist in him who feels revolted by the incongruity implicit in the picture of Shakara as a lover of Vasantasena. Therefore, even while campaigning so brilliantly in favour of his master in Act I, he experiences a sense of personal satisfaction when he comes to know that she was spurning all enticements because of her love for Charudatta, and helps her escape from the clutches of Shakara. This he does with no hope of personal gain; indeed, his professional prospects the other way should be far more alluring. He comes to her aid only because Vasantasena's union with Charudatta is an aesthetically satisfying proposition: it would be a 'fitting union of two gems'[7], as he says. The play of moral and aesthetic sentiments is thus a constant feature in the character of the Vita.

He is pulled in two contrary directions all along: his sense of duty and material prospects keep him tethered to Shakara, but his moral and aesthetic susceptibilities incline him towards the noble and indigent Charudatta. It is a pull between the demands of trade and art. There is, of course, not the slightest doubt in the mind of the spectator as to which of the two forces would gain predominance, but the dramatic excitement over the confrontation of values is kept alive by the manner in which Shudraka introduces it time and again in the character of the Vita, and presents it against both comic and tragic contexts in the play. The pleasure-garden scene in Act VIII furnishes the finest illustration of this collision of loyalties.

The scene opens with Vasantasena boarding a wrong carriage and, instead of the rendezvous fixed with Charudatta, reaching the spot where Shakara is diverting himself with his companions. The Vita is the first one to peep inside and discover her in the carriage. In shocked disbelief he stares at her for a few moments, thinking she was on a visitation to Shakara. He reflects ruefully on the gross incompatibility of the match,[8] but does not immediately voice his inner feelings. As a professional love-messenger he is somewhat cynical about women's love,[9] and, after all, in his role of an attendant to Shakara he can have no justification for expressing a feeling of disappointment. All the same, the demands of 'art' and 'trade' are in a state of acute conflict within him and all his pronouncements and gestures in this memorable scene are informed by the resultant tension.

To begin with, he softly mutters his disapproval of Vasantasena's conduct, telling her that she showed a lack of 'nobility' and consistency in first fleeing from Shakara and then returning to woo the same person, under pressure of her mother, for the sake of financial gain. Immediately, however, the professional in him takes over, and affably, though cynically, he comments:[10]

> Why, I did (formerly) say to you – O good maiden, you should impartially serve people irrespective of whether they attract or repel you.

But no sooner she protests her innocence and says she is there by accident and not by choice, he is anxious to whisk her away to safety. He fails in his attempt, no doubt; but the alacrity and zeal with which he volunteers to help her, even by running a grave personal risk, go to suggest an exceptional temperament in a Vita. Clearly, both in his disparaging asides in regard to Shakara and his joyous envisioning of the union of Ujjayni's *'nagara Sri'* with *'nagaryam tilakabhutam'*[11], his reactions are as much moral as aesthetic. One should compare the reactions of the Cheta and the Vita to the main events in the scene to appreciate the special quality about the latter. The Cheta talks in broadly human terms, and the sense of outrage he expresses on the strangling of Vasantasena is a moral reaction, but they have nothing of the aesthetic quality so distinct in the words[12] and acts of the Vita.

As the scene slowly advances to a horrible climax, the Vita is shown gradually shedding his professional mask and revealing his true character. The manner in which he champions Vasantasena's attachment to Charudatta, expresses his disapproval of her suspected change, laments her supposed death, and, finally, refuses to serve the hateful Shakara and chooses instead to join the rebel army, clearly indicate that an essentially artistic temperament imples him to perform these gallant, self-abnegating acts. To be sure, he keeps up his professional posture almost till the very end. For example, he offers resistance when Shakara tries to force *Vasantasena*, but when Shakara pleads with him to leave them alone for a few moments so that he might try to win her over with tender solicitation, the Vita sees he cannot really protest, and with a certain professional cynicism walks away some distance. But his final act of spurning Shakara and running away to the rebel camp convincingly demonstrates the triumph of his moral and artistic disposition over his professional, mercenary self. He has, all along, made a valiant effort to subserve to the demands of his trade without compromising his own personal set of values. But when 'trade' demands a total disregard of human values and emotions that he had nurtured with an artist's passion, when it compels decline into grossness, he chooses rather to sacrifice the trade itself and court a life of danger and insecurity.

King Palaka is not brought on the stage. But we are made to know of his vileness from what we hear in his proclamations and orders, and from the conduct of his protege, the barbarous Shakara. Ranged against this established order of primitive sensuality and gross material affluence, we have the opposite camp constituting a refined order of innocence, beauty, and tender sentiments. The uprising in the play does not have merely a political dimension; it also vindicates a refined order of art and morality against a gross order of material advancement and sensual appetite. The play is concerned with reorganisation of social order and individual life on the basis of certain aesthetic, liberal sentiments that facilitate fulfilment of joyous potentialities of life both at communal and personal levels. It is for this reason that the artistic disposition of most of the characters, primary and secondary, has been so often emphasized. Rebhila the musician (whom we do not see), Vasantasena and Charudatta the lovers, all the secondary characters except Shakara, and, finally, Aryaka, the new king, represent the ascendancy of refined sentiments over mundane interests and pulls. The motif attains a splendid consummation in the story of Vasantasena.

Vasantasena is one of the most captivating heroines in Sanskrit drama. As her name suggests, and as the play poetically underscores at several points, she represents the enchating possibilities of spring. She trades in love, but is no harlot; a sophisticated *ganika*, she is coveted for her culture, vivacity, good taste, elegance, and artistic accomplishments, and not merely for her extraordinary physical charms. She heads a huge establishment with a large retinue of attendants, musicians and receptionists, and has a mansion which with its seven courtyards and sprawling enclosures, as described in Act IV, vie in opulence with a royal palace. To all appearance, therefore, she has everything that life has to offer. But, in reality, she is a deeply discontented soul, pining for a life of fuller womanhood. The art of love in which she is an adept, and her artistic and feminine attainments have so far been instruments of material advancement. She now longs to convert them into instruments of a profounder emotional fulfillment. She is in quest of a love which would transform her life, ensuring social and moral elevation at the same time as it would satisfy her feminine longings and enrich her sensibility.

Charudatta embodies exciting possibilities of such a fulfilment. He is a high-souled noble of Ujjayini, noted for his moral excellence, generosity of spirit and artistic temperament-qualities that have resulted in his decline from a high state of prosperity to one of mortifying penury. But the reversal of fortune has in no way affected his righteouness and grace. Vasantasena cherishes a deep love for him, but has not had any opportunity of communicating her feelings. When the play begins, she is already a love-lorn woman, spurning all enticements of wealth and honour from other quarters and given over entirely to fond thoughts of Charudatta. It so happens that, one evening, seeking to escape from the clutches of Shakara who is in hot pursuit, she runs into the old mansion of Charudatta. She has then her first opportunity of observing him at close quarters and engaging him in talk. Conducting herself in a demure and polite manner she exploits this opportunity for a shrewd assessment of his feelings for her. Charudatta, who had some prior intimation of Vasantasena's love for him, is quite eager to respond, but feels inhibited because of his present indigence. With unerring insight Vasantasena gauges his mind and, prudently enough, decides to wait for some more time before revealing her feeling. She knows it would be necessary, first of all, to convince him of the genuineness of her passion and make him aware of the true nature of her longing. And, for all her infatuation, she would not force matters. Deftly creating an opportunity for a further meeting with him, therefore, she happily returns home.

A number of interesting vignettes are offered in course of the first four Acts to bring out the nature of Vasantasena's ardour and aspiration. Through wonderfully subtle and elegant strokes the fuller dimensions of her passion for Charudatta are slowly unfolded before the audience. It is important to note how, in his dramatisation of the possibilities of human happiness, Shudraka does not introduce a set of ideal values to the exclusion of immediate, earthly ones. In contravention of conventional puritan codes, the play tries to portray how sensual charm itself can be harnessed as a refined source of fulfilment. Vasantasena's passion emphatically includes a longing for amorous joys, but it is transformed into something far more fascinating by being manipulated only as a stage in a process that would ultimately lead to her final liberation, both socially and psychologically, from the trade into which she is born. For her, love is now an instrument of emancipation from a state of emotional deprivation and moral inferiority. She aspires to be not just a beloved, but a wedded wife of Charudatta's, and looks upon love as the means to an enriching human relationship, and not mere sexual gratification. Moreover, as the 'clay-cart' episode in Act VI so touchingly dramatises,[13] she also wishes her passion to consummate in the fuller glory of motherhood.

She is keenly conscious of the irony and incongruity of her longing in the context of the realities of her life. This poignant awareness is movingly conveyed through her soliloquies and dialogues in the first four Acts. Three more Acts pass before she has a second meeting with Charudatta. A supremely tender sequence is employed in the interval to unfold the drama of Vasantasena's inner hopes and fears in the privacy of her house. Her struggle against the obligations of her station in life, her search for unadulterated love, her quest of the true beauty of life against the background of a sordid set of mercenary, decadent values which threaten to keep her permanently enthralled, constitute the main subject of *Mrichchakatikam*. As already indicated, Shakara and Charudatta represent two opposed worlds: the world of trade which debases life, and the world of art which refines and elevates it. Keeping the personality of Vasantasena at the centre, the playwright offers a series of developing tensions to incisively dramatise the liberating potential of refined passion. The nobility of Charudatta and his indigence, together, are so often emphasized by the dramatist in order that the quality of Vasantasena's impulse – '*Ata eva Kamyate*' (declared twice, in Act II and V) – may be properly appreciated.

When this is understood to be the subject of the play, certain apparently ordinary elements take on a significant dramatic value. Since Vasantasena's love for Charudatta has to attain a higher fulfilment she sheds all ornamental and mercenary trappings. The first four Acts which gradually lead up to the union of the lovers are carefully designed to highlight the process in a variety of ways. Vasantasena's apprehensions over the prejudice her 'art' would naturally evoke in others by being associated with 'trade' is repeatedly suggested through a number of poignant situations and dialogues. More interestingly, intimations are furnished at four crucial stages of Vasantasena's relationship with Charudatta to emphasise the necessity for her to discard all artful enticements natural to her trade.

On the eve of her very first meeting with Charudatta the situation so develops that she has to remove her garland and anklets before she can enter his house.[14] Later, as she prepares to go on a visitation to Charudatta, she is shown rejecting all embellishments suggested by her attendant and going forward to express her love in a simple, spontaneous manner. Just before her union with Charudatta takes place, similarly, she has to remove her rich fineries and drape around herself a piece of ordinary cloth.[15] In the last scene of the play, again, when her reunion with Charudatta is dramatised,[16] and when a permanent relationship with him is legitimised by the king's orders, she is presented in a plain, unadorned state. Dhuta's ringing statement that her husband is her brightest ornament,[17] and that she needs no other embellishment, similarly underscores this opposition in the play between plainness and adornment. In fact, the dramatic justification for conveying the story of union after Act V through a series of the melodramatic situations spanning another five Acts inheres mainly in the fact that the playwright is demonstrating how love which liberates and blesses is one where, in place of the 'abhisarika'– image and sportive disposition presented in Act V and the beginning of Act VI, a sober, unostentatious, sedate approach to life as projected through the last scene is more appropriate and enabling.

The two climactic points in the play, at the fifth and tenth Acts, are designed to project two contrasted sets of values. One of these involves an approach to human passion that is at once moral and aesthetic, and the other is concerned with divestment of love of all elegant make-up. Together, they indicate the way joys of human life acquire fullness and mellowness. From art it is necessary to glean sentiment, elegance, refinement and aesthetic impulse. But if art is to serve a richer human life, and not to degenerate into mere trade, it would be necessary to peel off all its artificiality which are sanctioned by society on grounds of sophistication. Spontaneity and sophistication are both necessary; but spontaneity, not of the primitive kind, and sophistication, not of the affected sort. Thus the play dramatises a healthy fusion of art and life, and thereby shows how to enrich either.

One remembers many of the delightful touches that were introduced so casually and unostentatiously in the earlier scenes: Vasantasena smelling the jasmine-scented cloak of Charudatta and happily commenting to herself that he was still not averse to the pleasures of youth; Vasantasena dissuading Samvahaka from taking a precipitate decision to enter the holy order; Charudatta joyously recounting before Maitreya the enthralling charms of Rebhila's music; and a host of others. One also remembers scenes containing a more direct and extended celebration of the joys of life and references to the experience of anguish in their absence – in the middle Acts and the final Act, in particular – to realize how the playwright is not out to persuade the audience to spurn either riches, or sophistication, or amorous delights, as such. Even in his darkest days of alienation and indigence Charudatta continues to nurture his aesthetic sensibility. Vasantasena, similarly, is presented as a woman with a deep, overpowering impulse, and also as a supremely elegant person possessed of a highly refined taste. The contrasted figure of Shakara highlights the theme in the reverse; and shows how a life of brute passion, devoid of culture and aesthetic taste, grows more and more debased, repellent and sinister.

There are yet other thematic opposites organised into plot and characterization in this play. We have, for example, an interesting set of ironics and contrasts produced by the interplay of the themes of affluence and indigence. In the first half the obvious contrast is of Charudatta's decrepit mansion and Vasantasena's splendid palace. These two constitute the setting of the drama for its first five Acts during which the dramatist repeatedly refers to the magnificence and splendour of the one, and the dilapidated state of the other. But the emphasis is also ironical: in terms of moral and emotional quality, the poor state of Charudatta's household symbolizes enviable prosperity, and the splendid establishment of Vasantasena represents deprivation. But we are not offered a simplistic equation of poverty and virtue, and of riches and vice, for if affluence can be dangerous and suicidal as in the case of Shakara, poverty, too, can be demonralising and crippling, as in the case of Sarvilaka. If affluence is suffocating to Vasantasena, indigence is depressing and agonising to Charudatta. As in the case of other dualities, here, too, Shudraka orders the resolution only after portraying the interaction over an extended length of the play.

Attention has already been drawn to the suggestive manner in which values of simplicity and plainness have been projected through certain important situations in Vasantasena's life. A dramatic climax relating to the thematic confrontation between affluence and indigence is also organised with similar finesse and emotional appeal at the very centre of the play. Soon after Vasantasena's final and unequivocal rejection of 'trade' and acceptance of an elevating relationship of love is dramatised at the end of Act V, Shudraka introduces the illuminating clay-cart episode at the beginning of Act VI to drive home the message from yet another perspective. Not only is Vasantasena's gift then spurned by Dhuta (with the polite, but telling, disclaimer: 'my husband is my most precious ornament'), even the child Rohasena is shown instinctively recoiling from her generous presents and demonstrative affection. Thus is dramatically suggested that Vasantasena is yet to attain the simplicity and natural dignity of a Dhuta: her acceptance in that household, therefore, is still provisional. Rohasena reacts, first, at her costly jewellery, and, next, at her lack of composure, and protests that she does not at all resemble his mother. While this interlude enhances the sympathy of the audience for Vasantasena by a moving representation of her yearning for motherhood, it also *places* her. Rohasena's reactions suggest, at one level, Dhuta's reaction as well – it is by no means a hostile response, but not a cordial one either. The message is clear: Vasantasena can be admitted into their affections – that is to say, she can properly fulfil her aspiration – only on the basis of pure, natural, and noble impulses, as in the last Act, and not of glamour and sentiment as at present.

That, incidentally, gives us the cue to the real significance of the title[18] *The Clay-Cart.* A golden cart, the play seems to suggest, need not be frowned upon if it serves to support a refined order of life and does not contribute to vulgarisation and debasement. There is nothing of the puritan about the writer of *Mrichchakatikam*, but there is nothing of the dandy either. While he raises no objections against the golden cart as such, he does not hesitate to suggest that one is more likely to find a safer means of conveyance to the felicities of life in a plain and simple caly-cart. What the golden cart stands for may be welcome to the extent that it would make possible the leisured cultivation of arts and virtues, as indicated through references to Charudatta's earlier life. But, then, one must guard against frivolity and vulgar complacency which a leisured life may breed, and assiduously cultivate higher values and impulses. As the Vita comments, a pond with hygienic, sweet water is likely to dry up soon (like Charudatta), but is far more to be preferred to a stale and contaminated one where the water goes an accumulating to no end[19] (as with Shakara, or with Vasantasena's mother in the beginning). Ultimately, the value of a thing has to be determined by its viability as a means to a richer, more satisfying life. Shudraka is not a prudish, reactionary mind – he is not opposed to sex and riches in themselves; he welcomes them as things which make life more enjoyable, and rejects them only where they debase it.

As the mansions of Charudatta and Vasantasena constitute the background for the first six Acts, the pleasure-garden and execution-ground are the major settings for all but one of the later Acts. These settings, too, involve a fundamental irony: the pleasure-garden is the scene of brutish violence and murder, whereas the execution-ground is the place for the enactment of the story of emancipation and regeneration. As the tension between wealth and penury in the initial Acts is sorted out at aesthetic and emotional levels, so also in the final Acts a complementary duality and resolution is worked out. Instead of the contrast between Charudatta and Shakara that was earlier foregrounded, now the theme is amplified through the contrast between Charudatta and Samvahaka.

With a sudden change of fortune Charudatta regains in the last scene his lost riches and authority, and also his lady-love. He accepts the return of good fortune with humility but expresses his sense of joy in clear, unambiguous terms. Samvahaka the masseur, on the other hand, whose feeling of discontent had made him embrace the life of a Buddhist monk, reaffirms in the same scene his conviction that fulfillment of life can never be attained through worldly prosperities, and firmly rejects the authority and wealth offered to him. He is thus at the other extreme from Shakara, for whom sensual joys and riches constitute the highest felicity. Between the two extremes of vulgar affluence and ascetic renunciation, Charudatta and Vasantasena provide refined human approach to the wealth-penury opposition. [20]

Samvahaka-Charudatta contrast highlights yet another tension: worldliness versus other-worldliness. This is rather a surprising dramatic opposition to have in a play which so insistently and ardently advocates joys of human life. Both in style and theme so predominantly mundane, it yet introduces certain elements to set off the opposed values of renunciation and other-worldliness. Shudraka's Catholicism of taste and inclusiveness of perspective are reflected in his refusal to project the bliss of union achieved by Charudatta and Vasantasena as the only worthy vision of human happiness. He does not, to be sure, repudiate it with the bitter cynicism of a Malvolio or a Jacques. But he faithfully notes that a third vision is still possible, beyond the apparently exhaustive dualities of good and evil, comedy and poetry, trade and art, affluence and poverty, which he has brought into play and resolved with a bias for the wholesome joys of human life. He brings in, therefore, the Buddhistic vision of the world as a wheel of suffering, indicates the Vedantic direction of gaining absolute serenity and bliss, and also adumbrates a fatalistic vision of human life with Destiny controlling the entire chiaroscuro.

At the very beginning of the play, in the benedictory invocation itself, the opposition between love and renunciation, passion and void, life in *Prakriti* and life of the *Purusha*, are juxtaposed and fused by presenting, first, the picture of Lord Shiva in *nirvikalpa samadhi*, absorbed in the Great Void, and next, the contrasted picture of the same Lord Shiva in an amorous posture with His consort Gouri, the embodiment of *Prakriti*. The first involves total detachment, a state of complete self-sufficiency; the second shows a state of reaching out, of joyous union. If the second is intended to provide a key to the main *shringara rasa* of the play, the first would naturally suggest the highest form of *santa* in which ultimately everything finds its rest and fulfilment, and to which, according to Indian philosophy, all other experiences of life should serve as a stage and a process. Similarly, in the penultimate verse of the play – the one conveying Charudatta's philosophical reflections on destiny – a number of the earlier references to fate are gathered together and sounded to a final crescendo, counterbalancing the sense of fulfillment and joy issuing through the, lovers' union at the personal level, and the political reorganisation at the communal level. Both reversal and consummation are viewed as being equally inevitable, and equally temporary, underscoring a philosophical vision of life's verities:[21]

> It empties some and fills others; some it raises up and others it causes to go down, while some it keeps in anxious suspense; bringing home to the people this course of the world which consists of opposites mutually meeting together. Thus does Destiny play with all creatures, constantly dramatising the maxim of the water-wheel and the buckets.

As has already been stated, confrontation between values of sensuous enjoyment and Buddhistic renunciation is portrayed in the character of Samvahaka both at the initial and concluding stages of the play. What seemed on the earlier occasion a desperate, precipitate resolution comes off in the last Act as an attainment of philosophical maturity. The masseur who wanted to grow into a mendicant friar in Act II, we remember, had been solicitously cautioned by Vasantasena not to throw away, on a sudden impulse, all the delights of human life. While her words on that occasion revealed her own aspirations and values in a superbly controlled, manner, they also served to bring into focus the Great Crossing. Now as the play draws to a close, while a state of harmony and joy is shown descending all around, Samvahaka is invited to state his choice:

> Char – O Bhikshu, what would you like best?

> Sam – Having witnessed this impermanence (of things here below), of such kind, the great liking that I had for an ascetic's life has been intensified.

The very things that yield for the central protagonists a feeling of deep satisfaction, and fill their minds with exciting future possibilities, induce in the monk an intense realisation of their inconstancy and convince him that Buddhistic *nivritti* is the only answer to the problems of life. The playwright does not forcefully argue it out; he does not wish to negate the vision of human happiness he has carved out with the story of the union of Charudatta and Vasantasena – a vision, it may be remembered, which embraces sensuous, moral, and aesthetic values, and suggests a state of peace and harmony at the individual, domestic, and communal levels. No doubt, it is an exciting and glorious vision. Yet, in the interest of comprehensiveness of portrayal, Shudraka feels impelled to organise a brief but telling vignette, emphasising certain values which transcend the purely humanistic ones projected through most part of the play.

That *Mrichchakatikam* represents the high watermark of realism on the Sanskrit stage needs no emphasis. This has already received an abundance of critical comments and Western critics, in particular, have found in it something very germane, and have rated the play very high on that score. It is necessary to point out, however, that Shudraka's play is not confined to etching out life-like scene and furnishing plenty of natural dialogue. More importantly, it puts those in the service of a special aesthetic position and moral perspective. An urge for realism in the ordinary sense does not control the portrayal of life here. There might be a number of scenes which are pre-eminently realistic in treatment and inspiration. But scenes presenting life in an idealised, heightened style are still more numerous, and they constitute the heart of the play. What one actually witnesses is an extended interaction between realism and idealism, life and art, running through the entire play.

In exploring superior possibilities of human happiness Shudraka presents a continuous juxtaposition of values of pragmatism and idealism. He has, of course, incorporated a wide variety of realistic characters and situations, exhibiting a penchant for realism in Chaucerian or Shakespearean manner. But, at the same time, the central episodes in the play have been imbued with heightening of such an order that it cannot just be described as a realistic piece. Vasantasena's passion, Charudatta's personality, Dhutta's character, nay, even the actions and aspirations of secondary characters like Sarvilaka, Madanika and Samvahaka, are pitched on such an idealised plane that *realism* can hardly be a suitable descriptive term for the drama. On the other hand, idealisation is not of a fictive kind, introducing incredible action, or heroic sentiment and conduct. Even the melodrama in the final Act cannot in that sense be dismissed as unrealistic. Shudraka's effort at synthesizing the real and the ideal in envisioning possibilities of happiness in human life involves a corresponding fusion at the presentational and stylistic levels.

In presenting an integrated vision of the comic and the poetic, the playwright devises a recurrent pattern of joining together gay and solemn tones. In the dialogues of the characters, no matter which pair it is, one notices a continuous interplay of light banter and serious concern. Except for two melodramatic scenes, interaction of the light and the serious is noticeable all through the play, imparting to the development of action and character a superb thickness of texture. How pervasive and exciting this interplay is may be easily appreciated by consulting not only major scenes like the meeting between Charudatta and Vasantasena, but even such asparently casual dialogues as are exchanged between Vasantasena and her attendants in Acts II and IV. What we have is not merely a mechanical alternation of comic and serious scenes involving secondary and central characters respectively, as seen in many other plays; in *Mrichchakatikam*, the casual and solemn operate concurrently nearly all the time. For example, even so palpable and typical a comic figure as Maitreya has to wear his comic gusto, for the most part, as a shield against the sad and serious thought rising within him with overpowering force.

At the stylistic level, similarly, one finds Shudraka concurrently harnessing the dual modes of documentation and symbolisation, prose and poetry. Fusion of statement and metaphor result in an exciting dramatic communication. At the conclusion of Act I, for instance, we hear a verse recited by Charudatta,[22] which constitutes both a realistic description of landscape and a brilliant projection of mood and impulse. Following the use of a significant pun on *'sneha'* (meaning both *oil* and *affection*), words like 'mud' and 'milk' acquire symbolic value and build a delightful network of emotive and semantic suggestions. Similarly complex evocations are incorporated at a number of other places. One needs only to remember the use made of a host of references-shawl, moonlight, necklace, storm, clay-cart, and many other – to realise the dramatic power with which realistic delineation and symbolic projection have been integrated in the play.

The Induction itself provides clear indications of the tonal design. The solemnity and poetic fervour of the benedictory verses very soon give place to an irreverent exclamation of the stage-manager's : 'Enough of this verbiage'. The comment is, no doubt, conventional. But, as may be seen, it sets the tone for the entire scene. After making this remark the stage-manager himself grows rather high-serious and gives a long discourse. This, in turn, is followed by a comic interlude, something racy, earthy, and completely uninhibited and direct. Thus we find a certain repetition of a tonal pattern-solemn formality is first deflated through down-to-earth realism, then there is the recurrence of a serious mood which, in its turn, is punctured by a light, informal touch. This alternation of formal and informal styles, of solemn and earthy moods in the Induction, prepares the ground for a larger and more elaborate manipulation of alternating, opposed tones and values in the play proper. The stage-manager's resolve to switch over from formal, cultivated Sanskrit to a more easy and suitable colloquialism is thus significant. Apart from some fundamental critical and historical questions it might stimulate in respect of a possible reformation of dramatic style, or expansion of audience that might have occurred in the time of Shudraka, the immediate dramatic interest of this unusual introduction is clear: it suggests the playwright's intention of emphasising both an opposition and integration of values and perspectives.

It is necessary to remember-as has been earlier discussed that shudraka is neither rejecting nor adhering exclusively to any one of the two modes or values. His vision of human happiness is built upon a synthesis of the two approaches to life: pragmatic and aesthetic, realistic and idealistic, informal and sophisticated. And so he juxtaposes and balances both the connected styles and perspectives. Thus, for instance, Charudatta's aesthetic, aristocratic outlook on life is counterbalanced by the prudent, matter-of-fact approach of Maitreya who carries into the play the stage-manager's iconoclasm, his intolerance of poetic sentiments and his empiricism.

We see sudden delightful incursions of Maitreya's earthly humour into situations that are charged with sentiment, deflating the pressure, but not quite destroying the poetry[23] of it. Thus, while Charudatta and Vasantasena in the first Act bow to each other, high-strong and uneasy with the passion and embarrassment of first encounter, Maitreya solemnly mimics their gesture and says he is "like a half-grown camel bobbing his head between two verdant patches of rich corn, with their stalks bent under the wind".[24] One may see how his words effect dispersal of tension without spoiling the sentimental beauty of the occasion. The half-grown camel is, of course, brought in for sheer mirth, offering a grotesque caricature of the stiff and formal manner in which the lovers are bowing to each other. But there is also the other, counter balancing image of pure beauty. The poetic evocation contained in the graceful wavy movement of ricestalks- symbolising elegance, youthfulness and fertility – intensifies rather than disturbs the romantic mood. Maitreya's words beautifully unite the comic and the poetic and evoke both laughter and thrill in a chaste, elegant manner. Similarly, again, towards the end of Act V when emotional fervour in the lovers has attained its peak, and the approaching high-romantic consummation is prepared for with compelling lyricism, Maitreya's mock-innocent questions on the purpose of Vasantasena's visit and her plans for the night introduce a sharp anti-climactic earthliness into a rarefied situation. And here, too, comedy does not obstruct the movement into a deeper lyrical experience; rather it imparts a touch of reality, and enhances the appeal.

It is instructive to note how this endeavour at harnessing various dualities in respect of a number of themes controls the manipulation of both style and vision in the play. Contrasted elements such as personal and communal, contrived and accidental (for example, the progress of Vasantasena's ornaments in the early Acts as also at Act Nine), humanistic and fatalistic, are joined as closely fitting arcs to prepare the comic-poetic world of the play. More because of such thematic complexity and multivalence than of organisation of a number of episodes ('pataka' of the political revolution, and a number of *prakaris* relating to a variety of minor events), a vast gallery of dramatic personae, numerous vividly contrasted setting and situations, and the sprawling expanse of ten Acts, that *Mrichchakatikam* produces its impact of vast, versatile sweep and comprehensive portrayal. In the pursuit of a truly satisfying life, a life that is joyous, wholesome, and noble, it explores a variegated world full of dualities and contrasts. Without forcing antinomies and alternatives into some arbitary, contrived mould, it attempts to synthesize as many of them as possible and, for the rest, leaves the options open.

The play certainly upholds the Classical approach of the golden mean, but does not look askance at man's devotion to extreme values as long as that does not affect the sweetness and harmony of social life. Everything is welcomed: everything except evil and ugliness. As the verses at the two climactic points in the play-concluding ones in the supremely graceful fifth Act and the superbly melodramatic tenth Act-equally emphasize, the notes may be different, and the experiences may vary, but what ultimately emerges from their orchestration is an exquisite harmony, bringing about an unforgettable sense of joyous fulfillment all around:[25]

> Shrilly on the *tala* leaves; rumbling on the branches, harshly on stones and fiercely on the waters – thus do the showers fall, resembling lutes played upon in musical concern to the keeping of time. (V.52)
>
> May cows yield (plenty of) milk, the earth produce all kinds of grains in abundance, the clouds shower rains in due season, and the winds blow to gladden the hearts of all people. May all creatures always rejoice, the Brahmanas be ever respected, and the virtuous become rich. And may righteous kings subdue their foes and govern the earth.(X.61)

Notes and References

References to the text are from The *Mrichchakatikam*, M.R. Kale (ed.), Motilal Banarasidass, Varanasi, Third Revised Edition, 1972.

1. Shudraka's efforts at striking a balance between certain opposed themes have been noted. Thus, for instance, A.K.Warder (*Indian Kavya Literature*, Vol. III, Motilal Banarasidass, Delhi, First Edition, 1977 – Sections 1183 and 1211) talks of the theme of fate and free-will. But the range and multiplicity of the syntheses have not been adequately discussed yet. As Raymond Williams notes (*Modern Tragedy,* London, 1966, p. 24), transition from a metaphysical to a critical orientation is a natural development in the sphere of tragedy proper, too. But the centrality of the individual in a tragedy differentiates it from a tragi-comedy like *Mrichchakatikam* which is both individual and general in its orientation at the same time.
2. A.KWarder, op. cit., 1211.
3. *Mrichchakatikam*, Act II.
4. Ibid., III. 13.
5. For example, see, Theodore Goldstucker, *Sanskrit and Culture*, Indological Book House, Varanasi, 1971, p. 18.

   How erroneous it is to describe him as a "parasite" can be seen from the present discussion. Sylvain Levi is so impressed by this character as to eulogise him in very extraordinary terms and, in the process, commit a grave critical error:

   "The Vita is the most important character of all; we should almost say the only intelligent character of the Indian theatre".
6. Sylvain Levi, *The Theatre of India*, Vol. I, Writers' Workshop, Calcutta, 1978, p. 186.
7. *Mrichchakatikam*, Act I: "*Ratnam Ratnena Sangachchate*" (A jewel unites with a jewel – Tr. Kale, op.cit., p. 39).

8. Ibid., VIII. 16: (Seeing Vasantasena – sorrowfully to himself) – 'Ah! How is it that the doe is following a tiger! Oh, alas! –

   Leaving the male swan, resplendent like the autumnal moon and reclining on a stretch of (white) sand, the female swan has taken herself to a crow!' (Tr. Kale, op. cit., p. 271)

9. Ibid., VIII. 17 – *"Asaundiryam"*.

10. Ibid., I. 31. (*"Samupachara bhadre supriyam vapriyam va"*) "Embodiment of the prosperity and beauty of the city", and "the auspicious vermillion mark at the centre of the forehead".

12. *Mrichchakatikam*, VIII. 38:

    (Coming to himself, mournfully). 'O Vasantasena! the river of the water in the form of innocence is dried up. Love has departed to its original home! Alas, alas! O you who were an adornment of your ornaments, you with that sweet face..... you that were the river of goodness, with laughter for the sandy bank,.... Alas! Alas!....'

    (Tr. Kale, op. cit., p. 293)

13. Ibid., Act VI

14. Ibid., Act I.

15. Ibid., Act V.

16. Ibid., Act X.

17. Ibid., Act VI – (Aryaputra eva mamabharana-visesa yanatu bhavati.)

18. An extreme example may be cited:

    Srinivasa Sastri discusses the significance of the title and, in line with almost all other commentators of *Mrichchakatikam*, first of all, emphasises the importance – in terms of development of plot – of the jewels left in the clay- cart by Vasantasena. He quotes from Kantanath Sastri's *Mrichchakatikam Samikshya* and argues that the clay-cart signifies dangers of discontent and jealousy. This is, clearly, an untenable argument. One notes in this context his strange assertion that Charudatta was drawn towards Vasantasena because of his dissatisfaction with Dhuta, and that this caused all the misery – hence, he claims, the title suggests the feelings of discontent. There could hardly be a more exotic interpretation. See, Dr. Srinivas Sastri (ed.), *Mrichchakatikam*, Sahitya Bhandar, Meerut, Fourth Impression, 1976, pp. 16-7. Dr. Rangeya Raghav goes to another extreme by bringing in (in the Preface to his Hindi translation of the play) an allegory of the soul (in its clay-cart, i.e., physical body) to explain the title.

19. *Mrichchakatikam*. 46:

    "He has dried up by satisfying the thirst of men, like a reservoir full of water, in hot season."

    (Tr. Kale, op. cit., p. 51)

20. Critics who do not enquire into the deeper thematic implications of the play unjustly condemn the repetition of the motif, and some other central elements in the play:

    "It does not seem proper to decry poverty through nearly fifty-two verses and to discuss it at forty places (in the play). Is penury so reprehensible a thing?.... Personally, I would like to suggest that his (Charudatta's) scornful attitude against the state of indigence is in itself the cause of his fall from the exalted state of Brahmanhood. How wide, indeed, is the gulf between the state of a Brahmin and the joys of the brothel- house!" –

    Ramji Upadhyaya and Ram Gopal Misra, *Sanskrit Ke Mahakavi Aur Kavya*, Ramnarayallal Venimadhab, Allahabad, 1965, p. 117.

    The reiteration of a certain theme should have alerted these critics to look for some deeper significance. The second half of the passage betrays not only a fundamental misconception in respect of the personalities of Charudatta and Vasantasena, it also shows an inadequate critical interest in the traditional prescriptions relating to a mixed kind of *Prakarana* like *Mrichchakatikam*. Also the narrow, prudish approach is fundamentally at variance with the spirit and culture implicit in the play. Charudatta is not represented as a profligate or a lascivious person. The superb balance in Shudraka's representation has to be appreciated if one is to properly understand the play. As their further arguments reveal, the authors do not also correctly respond to dramatic stylisation.

    Similarly, Bhola Shankar Vyas (*Sanskrita Kavi Darsana*, Chowkhamba Vidyabhavan, Varanasi, 1968 – p. 290 & 296) reacts unjustly against Charudatta's laments on poverty, and against poetic stylisation at Act V.

21. *Mrichchakatikam*, X. 60 (M.R.Kale, op. cit, p. 407)

22. Ibid., I.57.

23. G.K.Bhat makes a neat assessment of Maitreya's clear-sightedness and matter-of-factness:

    "Maitreya turns his sharp satire to every inconsistency and shortcoming. Nothing seems to escape his observant and thoughtful eye. He does not exclude Charudatta or even himself from criticism. It is no wonder then that the entire creation figures in his witty similes. From the clod of earth to the heaven, from flowers to stars, from the inanimate creation to the animals and human beings, and from zoology to mythology, all things swim into his unchecked vision and supply the theme for his sharp and satirical humour." – G.K.Bhat, *The Vidusaka*, The New Order Book Co., Ahmedabad, 1959, p. 237.

    But the fact that Maitreya is also intrinsically in sympathy with poetic sentiments and higher ideals of life has to be adequately understood. Shudraka would not present a one-sided Vidusaka in a play like *Mrichchakatikam* which is a marvel of synthesis and balance.

24. *Mrichchakatikam*, I. 56(-).

25. Ibid., Kale op. cit., p. 213 and 407.

CHAPTER 4

Uttara Ramacharitam: Dramatic Design and Moral Perspective

Uttara Ramacharitam portrays an advanced state of civilisation and sensibility against a primeval, mythical backdrop. It incorporates into its action primal creative acts of Valmiki and Bharata, the first poet and first dramatist respectively in the Indian tradition[1], introducing an elemental human mode: man's mythical organisation of the forces of the universe he inhabits. In his introductory remarks in the play-within-the-play in the final Act the *sutradhara* narrates how the seer poet Valmiki induces all creation to witness the prophetic, poetic conjuration of a new order. The happy resolution at the end is shown issuing through a creative intervention of the poet-sage and not through some conventional accidents of fortune: the figurative description, *Kavireva Prajapati*,[2] is realised here as dramatic action. Commanding the obedience of all three worlds, the primal creative genius is shown reorganising private and communal destiny by imposing on the supernatural order and the refractory human world alike a superior moral pattern which he impels into being by stimulating and organising certain incipient potentialities of Nature, represented in the scene through Mother Earth and the Holy Ganges. The stage is converted for the moment into a microcosm reflecting a primal order where inanimate, animate and super-animate, the three *Gunas* and their various manifestations, are all brought into a state of harmonious co-existence.

This mythical restructuring of life is dramatised through recurrent naturalisation of fantasy[3]. Human and divine elements are made to intimately interact and merge with each other. Since the central characters represent both the orders-Rama and Sita being at the same time human and divine – this does not result in a feeling of artificial contrivance. Earth, air, water and fire assume physical forms and participate in the action. Woodland nymphs and river sylphs act as natural companions to the divine beings whose story in their incarnated, human forms is being dramatised. Magic weapons of stupefaction, of fire, fire, and of rain materialise with a certain elemental grandeur. But even today these do not stand out as far-fetched supernaturalism because the entire play is prepared in a suitable harmonious style. The *human* characters themselves being mythical, divine personalities, the distinction between mythological and naturalistic modes becomes irrelevant here.

In strictly dramatic terms, too, the distinction is rendered inoperative by a process of symbolisation and poetic evocation which keeps the play stationed at a rarefied plane throughout. Moreover, Bhavabhuti makes sustained use of an exotic, pastoral backdrop in order to naturalise the poetic-magical mode. Except for Act I which has the palace at Ayodhya for its setting, the entire story is dramatised against, a woodland backdrop. And even in Act I the consciousness of the characters, and through it of the spectators, is flooded with haunting evocations of the idyllic world of nature.[4] The power and virtuosity with which the environs of a pastoral world are almost ubiquitously conjured in the play leave no doubt in the mind that Bhavabhuti intends them to serve a central dramatic purpose.

Appropriately enough, an atmosphere of dream is made to preside over the entire length of the play without affecting the human immediacy of presentation. Dramatic significance of this pervasive dream atmosphere has received scant mention in critics of Bhavabhuti.[5] Few seem to have appreciated the fact that Bhavabhuti makes use of magical, pastoral, and dream-like situations in the play in order to establish in the mind of the spectator a particular state without which the nature of its poetic vision and the quality of its dramatic experience cannot be realised. The state is akin to precipitation of a deep inwardness while one's gaze is riveted on some external objects, a state which admits of the consciousness of *reality*, but only in an abstracted manner.

Of the many ways Bhavabhuti induces such a paradoxical state of sentience, dramatically one of the most effective is the supersession, or modification, of the ordinary time-process. The play is not so much an ordering of certain events in their natural sequence as a kind of kaleidoscopic documentary. The drama and its source- actions are repeatedly presented on a synchronic axis. Thus, for example, both the composition and the dramatisation of the *Ramayana* are presented together with the living actions of the characters Valmiki delineates in the epic – the final dramatic action constituting the conclusion of the epic being contemporaneous with its composition. Dramatic presentation is made to cohere with a kind of prophetic, creative time by constantly incorporating into the present both past and future and, at the same time, allowing the play to develop along its plot. The conclusion of the play issues from the womb of a play-within-the play which dramatises details of a past that had been concealed from Rama and others; and the happy resolution in the immediate present was a future already contrived by Valmiki earlier, as the introduction to Act VI makes clear. The play-within-the-play emerges as a coherent, effective dramatic device because in the Acts proper Bhavabhuti has so prepared dramatic action that successive movement of time is constantly altered, and a complex time-awareness is impressed in the mind of the spectator.

Drama here is not a time-bound succession of events in logical progression. For the most part, its *action* inheres in recapitulation and reflection. The larger part of Act I – the picture-gallery scene – is devoted to a reminiscence of past experiences. As they recaptitulate and re-live the past, both the central characters seem to lose their sense of present actuality; it is the past which now dominates and controls the present. So also does the future. All that happens on the stage in relation to present time foreshadows a future to which it is inexorably leading, the celebrated Bhavabhutian dramatic irony operating in its most extensive and poignant form to sustain this relation. Act II has a similar pattern. Its *Viskambhaka*, first of all, conveys certain vital information about the life of the main characters during the preceding twelve years (the time-gap between two Acts), then goes on to furnish other information that have a central bearing on the future Acts, and, thereafter, leads the spectators to the dramatic moment in the present. Rama is introduced on the stage and made to perform a brief initial action of punishing and liberating Shambuka. Thereafter, his consciousness is kept oscillating between the present and the past throughout the Act.

A similar pattern is repeated in Act III, this time with the further addition of powerful intimations of future. Contrasted to the one in Act II, the *Viskambhaka* here is more directly concerned with the events to come. The Act proper constitutes a brilliant telescoping of past, present and future into one undivided continuum in the minds of the main characters. Both Rama and Sita, placed on two different planes of reality, are repeatedly shown losing their sense of present actualities under the overwhelming stress of past memories and dark visions of the future. As the characters slide into states of stupor, speechless despair, or shattering mental agony, the drama lifts itself out of conventional engagement in *action* and plunges into a state of deep psychological interiorisation, effacing the ordinary divisions of time. The other *Acts*, similarly, project the present in an almost constant state of tension, stretched backward or forward all the time. Memory and desire repeatedly confound the sense of successive time. Act VII forms a natural climax in this respect, absorbing together the three dimension of time into a special order represented through the concretisation of poetic vision in the play-within-the-play.

But the play is not merely an exercise in cinematic techniques of flashback and prophecy.[6] It involves a more complex dramatic organisation. Through most part of the play its major characters are mentally removed from their immediate physical environs and kept suspended in an inner state, experiencing an undifferentiated co-presence of past, present and future. The dramatic 'present' has linked moments behind and ahead. A synthetic process of Bergsonian duree stretching itself continually into the future governs the enactment of dramatic experience. The aesthetic intention is to lead one beyond the transient *vibhavas* into the permanent seat of *rasa*, from temporality to permanence at the psychological level. In this sense, *Uttara Ramacharitam* marks a climax to the pure and unswerving pursuit of *rasa* in Sanskrit drama.

The purity and concentration in organisation of *rasa* gives us a key to the choice of the play's subject matter. *Uttara Ramcharitam* – the later history of Rama – it is clear, does not involve a conventional, uncritical adaptation of popular mythology. Bhavabhuti was, no doubt, trying to conform to Sanskrit dramatic tradition in opting for a subject from the epics. But he treated it in a wholly new-experimental fashion. An inadequate understanding of the novelty of its creative organisation seems to have been responsible for a variety of hasty judgements on the play. For instance, some extremely hostile reactions against the conclusion appear to stem from a simplistic approach to the constantly bitter-sweet mood of the play in conventional tragi-comic terms. D.L. Roy thinks it constitutes a complete sell-out of poetic justice, and I. Shekhar harshly comments that 'the fool of a dramatist' was stupidly trying to conform to convention. Such responses issue from a failure to recognise that Bhavabhuti was dramatising not a simple reunion, but universal harmony[8]. The novelty of the play, again, does not reside in merely certain obvious departures from Valmiki that continue to be avidly discussed by critics. More centrally. it is an aesthetic departure: mood rather than action, sentiment rather than character, constitute Bhavabhuti's main focus, and determine the style of his presentation.

For such a dramatic design there could be no better subject than Rama's later history, which is a prolonged study in mental agony without the relief of mighty engagements as in the *earlier* history, a point underscored in the play itself.[9] But action-obsessed critics bewail the absence of *action* in the middle Acts[10], not realising that action here is predominantly psychological and visionary in character. While events at the gross level pertaining to ordinary time are not copious, action at the deeper level of impulse and emotions arranged on a plane of duree and prophecy as noted earlier is organised extensively. This is further intensified by recurrent manipulation of dramatic irony. For example, each of the brief incidental dialogues in Act I, seemingly commonplace elements comprising formal communication, is in reality charged with dramatic anticipation. Moving on to Act VII one discovers how each such minute particular in the first Act is dramatically consummated at the end. So do the other Acts contain oblique dramatic suggestions in abundance. While these attest to the intellectual control and logical tautness of *Uttara Ramacharitam*, and help generate a rich theatrical experience at the surface level, they also subserve to a deeper aesthetic intent by reinforcing the suspension of consciousness of successive time. Taken in all, *Uttara Ramacharitam* is found to present a concentrated spell of interiorisation in which events occurring over long stretches of time are condensed and emotively crystallised into one dominant unit of experience.

Such a scheme would naturally result in a state of consciousness mid-way between reality and dream. A feeling of amazement and wonder, the experience of being precariously suspended between appearance and reality, is recurrently projected by Bhavabhuti in respect of most of the characters in the play in order that the dream-world atmosphere should be pervasive and gripping. We might very briefly recount this experience in respect of only one character, Rama. There is the picture-gallery scene in Act I, the long brooding reflection in Act II, the tantalising sensation of touching an invisible Sita and falling into swoons through intense re-experience in the Act III[11], an equally tantalising experience in the *Recognition Act* in the presence of Lava and Kusa, and, finally, in the last Act the state of regaining consciousness after a fit of fainting, and being left incredulous and dazed in the presence of a new reality. Numerous other small strands are inscribed in the portrayal of Rama to bring out the dreamy, fluid state of his mind through most part of the play.

Similarly, inadequate appreciation of Bhavabhuti's perspective and design has rendered certain critical reactions both inaccurate and inconsistent in respect of what are described as the play's supernatural elements'. Arguments against a supposedly excessive use of supernaturalism, or defence of its use, would be equally deviant in the context of a play like *Uttara Ramacharitam* which seeks to create a heightened mythical atmosphere, and seeks-as has been discussed-to obliterate distinctions between real and unreal, factual and fictive, natural and supernatural, distinctions that would have been acceptable neither to Valmiki nor to Bhavabhuti. And yet, one finds even sensitive, distinguished critics of the play exhibiting uneasiness over the mythic materials of the play-materials which they designate in conventional Western terms as supernatural.

We might refer to two of the more well-known critics of Sanskrit drama. G.K. Bhat says:[12]

> And though her invisible presence (Sita's in Act III) is a supernatural touch in this otherwise intensely human Act, its justification lies in its necessity for the dramatic problem.

Again,

> But Bhavabhuti softens the shades of divinity about these characters....But in this play Bhavabhuti has learned the lesson of art and has succeeded in transforming the unavoidable supernatural into a believable natural.

I. Shekhar, similarly, comments:[13]

> But despite a masterly characterisation and emotional treatment by Bhavabhuti, it is difficult to commiserate with Sita when the poet reminds us of her being a goddess and residing with divinities...

But, in reality, a cleavage between the natural and the supernatural obtains nowhere in the play. Bhavabhuti does not permit the spectator to carry in his mind a sense of dichotomy between the two worlds. As has already been said, for purposes of organising an appropriate dramatic medium for the prophetic vision, he introduces a kind of stylised realism where ordinary concepts of reality are no longer tenable. Supernaturalism in *Malati-Madhuvam* and mythical material in *Uttara Ramcharitam* are, thus, worlds apart. The latter attempts to be at the same time vivid and dreamy, concrete and magical, and in achieving this the puranic concepts relating to the connection between divine and human kingdoms come in handy,. In order that this could be dramatically worked out, however, a new mode of dramatic time is designed, and idyllic, dreamy, mythical elements are introduced in profusion.

Inability to respond to Bhavabhuti's stylised art results in various kinds of confusion. There is, for instance, a critical misgiving in regard to Bhavabhuti's moral vision in the paly. It is suggested that his extreme concentration on a specific emotion leaves out of view the fundamental issue of moral conflict involved in the subject of the play. Since the main focus of the play is to be on *rasa*, Bhavabhuti does, of course, put greater emphasis on emotional experience of moral conflict than on elaborate delineation through action. Ethical considerations in the age of Bhavabhuti were grounded upon certain classically established, accepted norms. He does not have to resort to a dialectical unfoldment of ethical conflict: instead, he has to dramatise an intense experience of collision of loyalties.

The stylisation adopted by the play may make it appear as if the dramalist is out to project sentiments to the exclusion of logic of thought. If that were so *Uttara Ramacharitam* with all its captivating dramatic style would still not measure up to the standards of a great classical play. As may be seen, however, the play makes insistent enquiries in respect of moral choices. Localising the play in an elemental, mythical context and projecting a stylised plane of higher reality, Bhavabhuti engages dramatic action on a complex body of moral and emotional states of being. A headlong clash of two equally compelling sets of values relating to public duty and personal allegiance forms the main-spring of the paly's action.

Ramachandra as King is obliged to act in a manner which is outrageously unjust as also excruciatigly painful at the personal level. He has to treacherously forsake his innocent queen, whom he calls 'the prosperity of my house', 'the sole blessing of the families of Janaka and Raghu'[14].And, as Valmiki says, the love he bears her transcends ordinary comprehension [15]:

> Sita was naturally dear to the high-souled Rama; but that dearness she increased by her own virtues; in the same way Rama was dearer than even life to Sita; but *their hearts alone knew their mutual affection.*

And, yet he has to pitilessly turn her out; knowing full-well the immaculate purity and nobility of her character, he has to behave as if she was a tainted, fallen creature. Helpless and bitter, he mourns:[16]

> Through you the worlds are holy, but unholy are the words of the people in regard to you. In you the world finds succour, but you will fall a helpless victim.

He is tormented with the memory of the epic stretch of agony Sita had to undergo during his period of banishment and the mortification she had to bear at the public trial by fire-ordeal on the alien soil of Lanka. She is now to be sent away into the forest in an advanced state of pregnancy, less than a year after her return to Ayodhya.[17] He is racked between duty and love, but through all his mental agony he is absolutely clear on one point: for Ramachandra the king, the custodian of public morals and servant of his people, banishment of Sita is an inescapable duty. An extraordinary combination of adamantine firmness and tender sensibility – Vasanti aptly describes him as '*Vajradapi kathorani, Mriduni kusumadapi*'[18]- Rama Shakes himself free with a supreme exercise of will-power and passes the deadly royal order. Thereafter, for almost the whole of the rest of the play, he consigns himself to an unending stretch of agony and lamentation.

In this context Henry W. Wells finds in the play 'absence... of any truly rational view of experience'[19], and goes on to elaborate:[20]

> So far as ancient Indian thought can divorce political from religious consideration, Rama's decision seems purely political. One would suppose it at least subject to debate. An analogous episode in Western drama would almost certainly lead to a prolonged discussion, with partisans arranged dramatically on two sides. But Rama's decision is a blind and instantaneous assumption, as if predestined and beyond argument or the reach of intellectual or moral appraisal. It is neither whole-heartedly endorsed, nor condemned, nor viewed skeptically. The ethical problem is wholly ignored. The playwright proceeds at once to what he deems his proper task, the emotional aspects of the situation.

It is surprising that Wells, who in his very handsomely appreciative study of *Uttara Ramacharitam* recognised that the playwright had deliberately kept the drama free of a 'problem-play' orientation, could yet make the complaint. Drama structured upon debate might achieve high eloquence and forensic excitement but would not conduce to the production of *rasa* in line with the Sanskrit tradition. Bhavabhuti's dramatisation is impeccable in that context. His effort is directed at enabling the spectator to experience certain emotions with a deep inwardness and to sensitive his perception of a moral-aesthetic complex at the emotional, not intellectual, level. And his refusal to engage the audience in a debate results from an ultimate clarity of the moral vision involved-as the source book, *Ramayana*, and the cultural history of his times testify. Thus even as he presents an almost unending spectacle of psychological distress, he remains undistrubed at the metaphysical level. One should note the several ways he indicates the provisional nature of the suffering. One might remember the clam assurance of the prologue:

> Manager : If this scandal were to reach the great king, then it would be very painful.
>
> Actor : The sages and the gods will by all means bring about what is good.

The benediction of Vasistha in Act I, similarly, is emphatically optimistic. His words are not to be taken as merely a piece of formal greeting; for Vasistha is a prophet, and if he maintains a tone of exaltation and hope[21], it certainly guarantees an ultimate good. In fact, the words in question are meant to be understood as a deliberate attempt by the prophet to buttress Sita's mind against her impending misfortune. As Rama puts in immediately after [22]

> the speech of ordinary good men follows (is in keeping with) facts (events); while facts follow the utterances of venerable sages.

Promise of filial consummation voiced by Vasistha and recaptured once and again through suggestive devices-for example, the superb symbolisation, in Act III, of the young tusker; the plants and animals tended by Sita during her sojourn in the forest- ultimately bears fruit with the birth of Lava and Kusa. The portrayal of their precocious heroism too sounds a positive note. Moreover, the ultimate reunion towards which *Uttara Ramachritam* steadily moves after the Second Act keeps the spectator insulated against an experience of tragedy. Thus, absence of debate neither creates a sense of incompleteness, nor does it rupture the spectator's anticipation of resolution, both of which would have been exceptionable features in an Indian Nataka.

This, however, by no means implies a facile or causal handling of the ethical question. If Rama had been shown acting in an unfeeling and precipitate[23] manner, that would indeed have constituted a grave limitation of the play; in that case the spectator's response to the central character would have been the reverse of what the Sanskrit playwright sets out to produce. But Rama's action, which would seem today unjust and revolting, was considered both inevitable and laudable in the context of the cultural and kingly ideals of Rama's world, as also Bhavabhuti's. The unforgettable words of Rama in answer to Vasistha's message, and the comment of Sita which follows, in Act I may be recalled:

> Rama : Has not the revered Vasistha sent me some command?

Astavakra : Please listen : 'We are detained on account of the sacrifice... You are still a youth and new is thy rule; be thou devoted to pleasing thy subjects, the glory arising from that is thy greatest wealth.'

Rama : As the revered Vasistha commands. Affection, mercy, and happiness, ray, even Janaki – I shall feel no pang in abandoning in order to propitiate the people.

Sita : Hence, indeed, is my lord (called) the noblest of Raghu's race.

A comparative analysis of the treatment of the story in Valmiki, Kalidasa and Bhababhuti goes to show that, of the three, Bhavabhuti's is the most tender and sensitive rendering.[24] With all his delicate handling, however, the act in question would still appear outrageous if it bore any traces of emotional and moral obtuseness, or, selfish longing for popular applause. Bhavabhuti assiduously keeps Rama secure against both the possible charges, and convincingly shows how his action has no motive other than the pursuit of kingly 'dharma', and how, in fact, it constitutes an agonising act of self-sacrifice for him.

Besides, it should be remembered, even in the absence of Bharata's injuctions, Bhavabhuti's audience could not have viewed Rama's action as 'political' in a narrow, secular sense. For the ancient Indian king, political duty constituted the highest *dharma*, a supreme religious act. As emphasised by the divine Ganga and sage Valmiki, Rama's kingly decision is unimpeachable from a moral standpoint. Bhavabhuti takes paints to underscore this on a number of occasions. Rama's reactions[25] on the fatal communication of Durmukha show the emotional and ethical implications of the situation in their full plenitude and intensity. He is keenly aware – no one more than he-that the expulsion of Sita is an unjust, cruel, tyrannical act, but for king Rama there is no option. In his bitterness of heart he blames his stars, utters pathetic protestations against the workings of a malignant fate, but retains unsullied his love and regard for the subjects who are the immediate cause of his woe. Though they are called 'mean' by some of the other characters, *Uttara Ramacharitam* ensures a generous approach to the critics in Rama's kingdom. This is effected mainly by harnessing in their favour Rama's unfailing sympathy and regard, which incidentally, is essential in the context of a play that does not seek to introduce conscious villainy into its plot. Rama's solicitude for the happiness of his subjects is so deep that, lest they should feel hurt by an implied accusation, he imposes on himself a severe discipline of never allowing his grief to surface and thus foregoes even the simple solace of lamentation.

There are a number of places where Rama expresses his concern for shielding his subjects.[29] He points out how the fire-trial, conducted far away from Ayodhya, could not possibly be credited by ordinary folk. His keenness to defend his subjects even as he expresses in the seclusion of the forest his unhappiness that some of them could not properly assess their noble queen, finds poignant expression (in Act III) when at the end of a prolonged and bitter lamentation, he cries out:[30]

> Ye worthy citizens and inhabitants in the country: ye would not like the queen as reported to me to remain in my house. Therefore I abandoned her like grass in the uninhabited forest, and did not even mourn for her; but these various objects long familiar to me move me; therefore, being helpless, I weep thus bitterly today; please forgive me.

As Act III also makes abundantly clear, Rama is a deeply alienated soul in his tragic suffering.[26] He has none to blame and a great deal to suffer in silence. Tamasa compares his state aptly to a boiling cauldron with a tight cover on it.[27] As she feelingly describes his position,[28]

> He has to govern this world according to law with a vigilant mind; sorrow for his beloved withers his heart as heat a flower; as he himself repudiated thee, it is hard for him to seek relief from sorrow by weeping....

Sita is, of course, pure and blameless. But the subjects, too, are to be viewed with generous understanding, as the Holy Ganga herself affirms later.[31] Who, then, is morally responsible for what appears to be a wholly tragic development? It is not possible to allot the blame to any particular person. At one point in Act III, therefore, Tamasa says, it has to be understood as a mysterious decree of Destiny, and, as the Holy Ganga emphasises, Rama simply did not have any other choice. Bhavabhuti, however, does not leave it at that. He insists on examining the issue from all possible angles.[32] While Rama's sensitive, compassionate and just reactions are all very feelingly brought out, the dramatist does not allow him a moment's respite.

No one is made more keenly conscious than Rama of the element of personal betrayal. And in the context of this particular action, all his dependents and relations are shown to be emotionally estranged from him. Even Sita, who appears on the stage in Act III, has not entirely forgiven her dear lord. Her brief plaints, in Act III and Act VII, constitute possibly the most deeply piercing remarks against the king. In addition, Bhavabhuti brings in an ultimate possible censure from the private perspective through the mouth of Vasanti, the woodland goddess, who was a dear companion to Sita during her sojourn in the forest:[33]

> 'Thou art my life, thou art my second heart, thou art the moonlight of my eyes, thou art ambrosia to my body' – with these and hundreds of such sugared words having flattered that artless one – that very one thou – but enough, what need of more talk?

Again,[34]

> Oh, hard-hearted one, fame they say, is dear to thee; but can any infamy be more dreadful than this? What became of the fawn-eyed one in the forest?

To which crushing accusation Rama can only answer in a pathetic, unprotesting, distressed tone:

> Friend, what else could I think? Her creeper-like body resembling a soft and tender lotus, as if it were composed of moonlight, was torn to pieces by wild beasts, when she moved slowly on account of the throbbing burden of her womb, her eyes rolling like those of a timid fawn but one year old.

Rama cannot simply forgive himself. Fame, clearly, is not what he coveted. He considers himself a very *chandala*, the lowest of men for having done the deed. Reputation was a consideration, no doubt, but it was the reputation of the solar race-not his own-which he had taken into account. His station in life made such an act obligatory, but as an individual he never thought he merited the slightest clemency. On his very first appearance, twelve years after he had banished Sita, he is again shown performing a cruel piece of public duty, one from which as a private individual he would recoil in horror. The antithetical impulses which agitated his heart at the time of Sita's exile are brought home, once again, with superb dramatic power:[35]

> Oh, right hand. Let fall the sword on the *shudra* ascetic, that it may revive the dead Brahmana boy. Thou art a limb of Rama, able to banish Sita, exhausted by her heavy foetus; whence canst thou then have pity?

Thus, to say that *Uttara Ramacharitam* ignores the ethical question is to accept European ideas of ethical conflict, which seem to have weighed with some Indian critics as well.[36] Bhavabhuti was dramatising, not a political theme, but the clash of opposed values and duties operating at public and private levels. In spite of the traditional sanction behind the ethical vision as he portrays it, and with full assurance that his audience shared it, he still examines it in severely critical, and movingly human, terms. Neither allowing a complacent, self-righteous endorsement, nor arguing for a violent condemnation of the action, he maintains a neat ethical balance, and manages to ensure a deep measure of sympathy for all the characters. He provides occasions and perspectives where both these extreme responses could appear natural and valid. In the process he reveals, as all great artists have done, how our conventional, simplistic notions of right and wrong become wholly untenable in the context of certain complex human situations.

It is one of the major excellences of *Uttara Ramacharitam* that it presents a complex, intriguing moral question in all its ramifications and ambivalence without resorting to the commonplace device of introducing elements of selfishness, egotism or perversity. There is no simple and easy resolution available to a morally steadfast being, and, as the *Gita* says, even sages are confounded while determining right action.[37] *Uttara Ramacharitam*, of course, has no fundamental ethical ambiguity – as has been said earlier, both the Indian cultural and ethical traditions and the Sanskrit dramatic conventions keep it insured. All the same, preoccupation with ethical complexities constitutes a centre of attraction in the play. All possible emotional responses to the main action have been dramatised, and the points of view of a wide variety of characters are projected in the interest of a comprehensive judgement.

A Western playwright would have introduced debate and conflict of a more palpable kind. Indignation, revenge, violent hysteria – such might have been the focus of his treatment of Rama's act of forsaking Sita and its consequences. He would have produced in that case another *Medea* or *The Winter's Tale*, but not *Uttara Ramacharitam*, where rejection serves only to intensify the sense of attachment, and betrayal reinforces allegiance even at the very moment of its execution.

One might in this context take note of the treatment of moral complexity in *Hamlet. Uttara Ramacharitam,* too, presents a complex moral and psychological situation, but here the portrayal is of an altogether different order. Moral complexity that issues from the very nature of things, and not derived from a particular temperament, the kind of complexity that characterizes, 'what a piece of work is man?' manifests itself only fitfully and peripherally about the main action in *Hamlet*, and may be said to relate more to the Renaissance – mind than to the protagonist's. Philosophical flashes such as, 'there is Providence in the fall of a sparrow' and 'readiness is all' carry a load the character cannot really bear. The tension is not between two equally compelling, but opposed, ethical perceptions. Classical dissatisfactions on *Hamlet*, as also later ones as those of T.S. Eliot and L.C. knights do have a point.[38]

Complexity in *Uttara Ramacharitam* is an aesthetically of superior order. It has for its dramatic support characters who are mature, virtuous and noble, and who display a consistently optimistic and healthy outlook on life. The world they inhabit is a goodly one; nowhere through the bitter odyssey of their life do they question the fundamental beauty and wholesomeness of life. And yet tragedy strikes. A robust mind is now threatened with imbalance and despondency, exposed to an unresolvable set of opposed values. But there is no *disillusionment* in the standard Western, or Hamletian, sense. Rama continues to serve his subjects loyally, and cherish them fondly, even as he is agonised by the task of 'propitiating' them. In spite of the immensity of his grief, not for once does he grow solipsistic and treat the world as an evil thing. In fact, though the beauty and joy in the world outside becomes a factor to aggravate his grief, he keeps his aesthetic sensibility unaffected and continues to display a rich sensitivity all through the play.

So also does Janaka, aptly compared to a huge old tree with a smouldering fire within. Appearing gaunt and massive, he is hollowed out from inside through continuous grief on account of his daughter's misfortune. This has made him acutely, forbiddingly sensitive. But he never abandons his innate generosity of disposition. The sarcastic remarks he flings at Kausalya in the bitterness of his heart are followed by tender memories of their past friendship and mutual regard; his wrath against Rama quickly melts into sympathy; his fierce invectives against the people who are the cause of Sita's banishment give place to a soft murmur of kindliness. He would, he says in a moment of towering fury, either curse or crush Rama's kingdom; the next moment he explains how he can do neither, for Rama is still an adored son and the citizenry is composed of people who deservebity.[39]

Bitterness does not necessarily lead to violent cynicism or reckless action. One encounters a similar balance and measure in the behavior of Vasanti and Mother Earth. They experience intense pain, and they refuse to accept it with fatalistic meekness, but their sense of outrage does not cause them to question the fundamental order of things. They are pitched into the middle of two equally compelling sets of values, but the resulting tension and ambiguity are of a rarefied kind, unconnected with elements pertaining to gross material iniquities or personal fortune. The tragic complication becomes all the more profound and arresting because it is not based on the easy premise of individual depravity or villainy. All are essentially good, yet suffering ensues. The value-judgements are nowhere befuddled or obscured inspite of ambivalence of emotional pull.

Bhavabhuti does not focus the attention of his audience on problems of life in their intellectual configuration or on material events as such. The deployment of action in *Uttara Ramacharitam* is so conducted as to return, once and again, to the dominant *rasa* of *Karuna* [40] with a brilliant counterpointing introduced through diverse characters and subsidiary emotions. The dominant *rasa* of *Ramayana*, as Anandavardhana commented, and as Valmiki in *Uttara Ramacharitam* mentions, is *karuna*. The last canto of the epic which is being dramatised here is, in particular, saturated with *karuna*. The emotion of grief is provided a treatment that is lyrical in depth and epic in scope.[41] The manifold variations, the precise dramatic calibration of various degrees and nuances of *karuna* are superbly orchestrated. As Tamasa, describing the events of Act III which forms a climax, says:[42]

> Oh, wonderful is the chain of events (arrangement of incidents). The sentiment of pathos, though one in itself, being modified by various occasions, seems to assume different forms, as it were, as water assumes various modifications of eddies, bubbles, and waves and is nevertheless the same water.

The versatility and power of Bhavabhuti as a dramatist is well attested by the fact that the same emotion, occupying a major place in all the seven Acts of the play, is never for once felt to be repetitive and stereotyped. The playwright delineates *karuna* through every conceivable perspective : conjugal love (Rama and Sita), filial love (Janaka, Kausalya, Rama, Sita, Mother Earth, Ganga), comraderie (Vasanti) neighbourly fondness (Tamasa, Murala) brotherly love (Laksmana), feudal devotion (Durmukha, Sumantra and the Chamberlaine), and saintly kindliness with a touch of the filial (Valmiki, Vasistha, Arundhati). And these are employed in a multitude of forms encompassing the different orders of nature, humanity and divinity. Ultimately, therefore, the play emerges as a compact concretisation of the limitless possibilities of *karuna*. The wide spectrum of characterisation in the process goes to reveal Bhavabhuti's extraordinary dramatic reach. Unageing divinities like Ganga, ancient sages like Valmiki, a senior patriarch like Janaka, the royal mother Kausalya, adult protagonists, young adolescents comprising the heroic twins and their delightful companions, old domestics in the royal household-all of them are portrayed with unerring propriety and precision. Two of the subsidiary characters presented in Act III, who are apparently very much alike and who would not be expected to command much attention of the playwright, namely, the woodland goddess Vasanti and the river deity Tamasa, may be closely observed to appreciate Bhavabhuti's masterful characterisation.

Vasanti exhibits a far deeper distress on Sita's banishment than does Tamasa. The difference is warranted by considerations of dramatic propriety. For one thing, Vasanti has been pictured as a friend of Sita's;

also she has just learnt of the misfortune and humiliation suffered by her esteemed friend; and, further, uncertain about the fate of Sita after the banishment, she naturally apprehends the very worst. Her grief and resentment, therefore, know no measure. Though reverential towards Rama, she is also harsh and bitter in her rejoinders to him. She is shown oscillating between two contrasted emotions of sympathy and satire, understanding and indignation, displaying a moving human quality. This integration of antithetical moods generates a fine poetic tension: emotionally how compelling this can be may be seen even from ordinary expressions such as her words of address to Rama in *Verse 27- 'Ayi Kathora'* and *'Natha.'*

Tamasa, in contrast, is endowed with grace and composure of a superior kind; she possesses greater sympathetic insight into mental states of different characters. With a fine sense of dramatic contrast, Bhavabhuti brings her off as a mature person displaying far greater restraint and objectivity than Vasanti. The way she offers compact, choric comments on the predicament of Rama, and on the emotions experienced by Sita; supports Sita through a very difficult state of emotional turbulence, and generally preserves a balanced perspective on the issue at hand, reveals her maturity. This is quite in keeping with her role in the play-that of a motherly chaperone to Sita, as different from a friend like Vasanti.

Bhavabhuti's critical control is manifested in a variety of ways. Each verse involves some new modification, some special realisation of the central sentiment. Seemingly similar, they operate in ever-varying patterns and circles, each in its orbit, but drawn centripetally to the very same core. Thus are ensured both concentration and opulence. The subtle shades and nuances with which major psychological and emotional states are handled, and the minutely analytical and concrete manner in which they are detailed out, involve a constant intellectual control.

Act III is remarkable in this regard in its use of counterpoint, management of dramatic irony, parallelism, contrast, and dexterous variation of tone in providing an extended, moving portrayal of the sufferings Rama and Sita go through. Even a random sampling of apparently similar lamentations would bring home the subtleties of dramatic evocation. The three following extracts, for instance, appear very similar but reveal superb distinctiveness and aptness in their different contexts.[43]

> Alas! The world of living beings is now turned upside down; the purpose of Rama's life is at an end today. The earth is now a sterile withered wilderness; worldly life is without interest; full of worry is the self. I have no refuge left. What course is open to me?
>
> x x x x x
>
> My grief having become intense distracts me as if it were fresh, like fierce poison – juice after a long time violently bursting forth and circulating; like a splinter of an arrow shaken with force due to some cause or the other; like an ulcer, the mouth of which had been closed up, reopening in the centre of my heart.
>
> x x x x x
>
> Alas! Queen! My heart is bursting, the frame of my body is falling asunder; I think the world to be a void, I burn within with thick flames, my helpless soul sinks and is, as it were, engulfed in pitchy darkness; and distraction paralyses me from all sides.

Bhavabhuti's intellectual control is revealed in its most splendid form in the structural arrangement. The seven Acts of the play have been designed with a classical massiveness and simplicity. Although events spreading over a number of years are being dramatised with the aid of a multitude of characters, each alive in his own distinct way, the Acts are never for a moment clogged; one does not experience anywhere the feeling of intricate handling as in Elizabethan drama. The stage is never crowded with action, but clear development of a many-faceted dramatic plot is nowhere disturbed. Moreover, emphasis is invariably put on dramatically more promising items in the original story. Bhavabhuti's modifications of source are too well-known to be recounted; it is only necessary here to underline the fact that a discriminating intelligence is consistently at work. The intellectual control manifests itself in matters of dramatic organisation[44] as well. The script bears cues for all the necessary dramatic connections and for the logic of events and characterisation. For example, numerous tentacular references are thrown up by the dialogues in Act I, but the rich dramatic haul they contain is brought to light only in later Acts, particularly Act VII.

So close-knit, indeed, are its manifold strands that discussion of any particular element demands a comprehensive survey of the whole. The play is built through the interaction of a number of linked devices and ideas; and the links are so clearly manipulated that a critic needs to undergo no exertion in discovering the significant patterns of dramatic organisation. This, of course, does not mean that Bhavabhuti's art is either ostentatious or mechanical; it only shows how competently it looks after the theatrical need of clear communication. Widely divergent critical interpretations, as are found on many plays of Shakespeare are unthinkable in the case of *Uttara Ramacharitam.* Organisation, symbolisation, significant perspectives, interpretation of moods – the playwright himself has introduced relevant keys in respect of all these elements, and has consummated them with such power and felicity that outside critical aid appears to be all-but-redundant.

Notes and References

References to the text are from *Uttara Ramacharitam*, edited and translated by P.V.Kane and C.N.Joshi, Banarasidass, Fifth Edition, 1971.

1. In Act II Atreyi informs Vasanti of the miraculous acquisition of poetic powers by Valmiki. She also states that the sage was engaged at the time in composing the first epic, *Ramayana*, dealing with the life of Rama. Thus, composition of a part of the epic is concurrent with the events being described, while another part, as Act VII makes clear, is prophetically organised in advance of the event. Lava in Act IV announces that, in accordance with Valmiki's instructions, Sage Bharata was preparing a play-let based on the final event of the *Ramayana* (which is yet to take place) – this would be inscribed into Act VII as the climax of the drama, the play-within-the play.
2. 'The poet is a veritable Creator'- – *Agnipurana,* 345-10.
3. A brief spell of earthly realism which is organised at Act VI is confined to the introductory scene, the *Viskambhaka*, which has a separate kind of status in the play; it is peripheral to the main drama.
4. So compelling is this pressure that it engenders in Sita a 'dohada"(acute longing which is experienced by pregnant women) to visit the same forests.
5. R.D.Karmarkar's pejorative comment that Act III is like a fanciful dream may be taken as a representative view. See, R.D.Karmarkar, *Bhavabhuti*, Karnatak University, Dharwar, 1971, pp. 60 & 63.
6. H.W.Wells (*The Classical Drama of India*, Asia Publishing House, 1963, p. 184) says – "the greater part of the play.... deals with memory and prophecy". The emphasis in his *Six Sanskrit Plays* (Asia Publishing House, 1964, p. 354) is more to the point: "Time itself is wholly fluid"...etc.
7. L.Shekhar, *Sanskrit Drama: Its Origin and Decline*, Leiden, 1960, p. 169.

   S.K.De is right in emphasizing in this context that "the denouement of happy ending is not here a mere observance of convention, brought about in a forced way", and that "no other conclusion is possible from the poet's skilful readjustment of motives and incidents", though he does not explain the nature of the readjustment. See, S.N.Dasgupta and S.K.De, *A History of Sanskrit Literature* (Vol. 1), University of Calcutta, Second Edition, 1977, p. 294.
8. Even very sensitive critics of the play can go wrong by concentrating on the events (and the themes they involve) rather than on the more inclusive pattern of atmosphere, *rasa* and prophetic vision. For example, Amiya Dev suggests a

fundamentally similar scheme in respect of all these plays: "With the hero's recognition of this tragedy a period of suffering ensues. Through this suffering comes spiritual regeneration which qualifies him for a restoration to prosperity" (Tragi-comic suffering in *Shakuntala, Uttara Ramacharilam, Cymbeline* and *The Winter's Tale*", Jadavpur Journal of Comparative Literature, Vol. 8,1968, p. 50).

This is an obvious extension of the familiar Shakespearean pattern to embrace *Uttara Ramacharitam*, but the question of "spiritual regeneration", possibly valid in respect of a Leontes, seems to be altogether out of place in the context of a Ramachandra.

9. Towards the conclusion of Act III, for example, Rama explains to Vasanti:

   That former separation from the fair-eyed one, which produced.... the combats of warriors in which were constant incidents causing diversion, assuredly ended in the slaughter of my enemies through the use of remedies; but how is this present irremediable separation to be borne without complaining?

10. Not to speak of Western critics like Winternitz and Macdonell who began the vogue, such critics are legion in India, too. One may refer to some of the famous ones:

    Bhola Shankar Vyas (*Sanskrita Kavi Darsana*, Chowkhamba Vidyabhavan, Varanasi, 1955, p. 393) concludes that *Uttara Ramacharitam* is distinguished as a lyrical dance- drama, not as a drama proper.

    S.V.Dixit says (*Bhavabhuti: His life and literature*, Belgaum, 1958, p. 56): 'His plays are heavy for the stage. They lack swift and flowing action'

    R.D.Karmarkar thinks (*Bhavabhuti*, Karnatak University, Dharwar, 1971, p. 56): 'We think, therefore, that it is fair to admit that the *Uttara* has no plot as such.... (epics) a dramatic poem, rather than a drama?'

    Suryakant thinks ('Sanskrita Ke Pramukh Natyakar', *Bharatiya Natya Sahitya*, Ed. Dr. Nagendra, S. Chand & Co., Delhi, 1968, p.244) that Bhavabhuti is 'more a learned dramatist (learned in dramatics) than an excellent dramatist'.

    Dwijendra Lal Roy discusses (*Kalidasa Aur Bhavabhuti*, Hindi Grantha Ratnakar Private Ltd., Bombay, Second Edition, 1956) Bhavabhuti's dramatic qualities ('natakatva') and concludes that Act II, III, IV & VI in *Uttara Ramacharitam* are altogether "irrelevant" as far as 'action' is concerned. Sita's banishment, he asserts, is the only action in the play.

11. Strongly reminiscent of the dream-Act in Bhasa's *Svapna Vasavadattam.*

12. G.K.Bhat, *Bhavabhuti's Uttara Ramacharitam*, Popular Publishing House, Surat, Second Edition, 1965,pp. 72and 132-134.

13. I.Shekhar, op. cit., p. 144.

14. *Uttara Ramacharitam*, I. 38 & I. 51.

15. Ibid., VI. 31-32.

16. Ibid., I. 43.

17. *Uttara Ramacharitam* makes it a gap of only one or two months, thereby committing a "grave blunder in plot-construction", according to Mirashi.

Valmiki's *Ramayana* states that, before Sita was banished, Rama and Sita spent "a long time" in conjugal joy after their return from Lanka. See, V.V.Mirashi, Bhavabhuti, Motilal Banarasidass, 1974, pp. 266-7.

18. Harder than the thunderbolt, yet softer than a flower.
19. H.W.Wells, *The Classical Drama of India*, p. 168.
20. Ibid., p. 169.
21. *Uttara Ramacharitam*, 1.9.
22. Ibid., 1.10.
23. V.V.Mirashi (op. cit., pp. 274-5) offers a long drawn-out argument to establish Rama's "imprudence" and "thoughtless action". His major arguments appear to be based on suppositions of doubtful validity. The following arguments may be offered by way of correction:

    (i) Rama did not enquire about Sita's fate after the banishment because, as king, he was to maintain a total aloofness. One may refer to Act I where he considers it proper to offer apology to his subjects merely because he was lamenting her loss in the seclusion of the forest. He had to demonstrate that his sacrifice was complete and unqualified.

    (ii) Rama's lament that she must have been devoured by some beast of prey was merely expressive of his worst fears in regard to Sita: that he "believed" it to be so is a misreading.

    (iii) Janaka describes Rama's conduct as "hastiness" ("Kshiprakarita").

    True, but does the play so affirm? It was natural for Janaka, as a bereaved father, to make the comment. In any case, this is, at best, a point of view. The play has several others.

    (iv) It seems preposterous to extrapolate from Vasistha's message to Rama in Act I ("you are still very young and new to the administration of the kingdom") that the "sage had a suspicion" that Rama might act recklessly. Vasistha was only offering a very general and formal kind of advice. If at all some guess-work is permissible in this regard, it would be more correct to assert that, with his prophetic vision and comprehensive understanding of destiny and human action, the venerable sage could not have made any pejorative remarks against Rama.

    (v) Atreyi's answer, similarly, is only a rejoinder to Vasanti, on the latter's making an observation that it was incredible that Rama was permitted by the elders to do such a thing. Atreyi's words bear no other trace of critical overtones as supposed by Mirashi.

    (vi) Finally, Mirashi's conclusion – "So Bhavabhuti also thought that it was a thoughtless action of Rama" – is not borne out by the play.
24. A.P.Singh (*Bhavabhuti Aur Unki Natyakala*, Motilal Banarasidass, 1969, pp 167-180) presents a comparative assessment of the manner in which the problem is treated in Valmiki, Kalidasa and Bhavabhuti. Bhavabhuti's is shown to be the most human of the three.
25. *Uttara Ramacharitam*, 1,40-43.

26. Briefly touched by Krishna Chaitanya (*A New History of Sanskrit Literature*, Second Edition, Manohar, 1977, p. 338).
27. *Uttara Ramacharitam*, III 1.
28. Ibid., III. 30.
29. This, along with the main action of Sita's banishment, has been misunderstood by some as a populist overture by Rama. In a recent "critical" edition of *Uttara Ramacharitam*, the editors develop a strange thesis to claim that Vasistha is a target of the play's satire on account of his being a counsellor of populist governance and that Rama's populist posture causes a certain degeneration in respect of personal values, and organises the seed of *Karuna*; they believe that the dramatic thesis relates to a correction of such populist values. They further suggest that the dramatic exclamation conveying Rama's sense of disbelief at the end of the play – *Sarvamidam anubhavam nayita pratyeti* – emphasises Rama's critical view of his subjects.

    See, R.A. Pandeya and R.N. Mishra (ed.) (*Uttara Ramacharitam*, University Publications, Varanasi, 1977, pp. 4 & 7-10.
30. *Uttara Ramacharitam*, III, 32.
31. Ibid.,VII.6.
32. As S.V. Dixit says:

    '*Uttara Ramacharitam* is a veritable symposium on Sita-tyaga',

    (*Bhavabhuti* : *His Life and Literature*, Belgaum, 1958, P. 54).
33. *Uttara Ramacharitam*, III. 26.
34. Ibid., III. 27.
35. Ibid., II. 10.
36. For instance, D.L.Roy's assertion (*Kalidas Aur Bhavabhuti*, op. cit., pp. 24-26) that Bhavabhuti has "murdered poetic-justice" derives from a mistaken notion about Rama's conduct.
37. "Kim Karma Kimakarmoti Kavayo-pyatra mohita" – *Bhagavad Gita,* IV. 26.
38. See, T.S.Eliot, *Selected Essays*, Faber and Faber Ltd., London, Reprinted 1966, pp. 145-6; and L.C.Knights, *Explorations*, Chatto and Windus, London, Fourth Impression, 1963, pp. 67-71.
39. *Uttara Ramacharitam*, IV. 24.
40. Sanskrit commentators differ on the interpretation of the *Karuna rasa* present here.

    One might see a standard discussion of the problem in *Uttara Ramacharitam*, Ananda-Svarup (ed.), Motilal Banarasidass, Delhi, 1977, pp. 30-31.
41. Valdev Upadhyaya (*Sanskrita Sahitya Ka Itihas*, Vol. I, Sarada Samsthana, Varanasi, 1973, p. 545) finds in *Uttara Ramacharitam* qualities of a lyric-drama because of its tender depiction of emotion, and of an epic drama because of its "Classical" delineation of nature and battles.

42. *Uttara Ramacharitam*, III, 47. Among others, Mirashi seeks to correct the mistaken generalisations extrapolated from the verse by a number of commentators on a supposed 'rasa-theory' of Bhavabhuti, namely, that *Karuna* is the one and dominant dramatic rasa, or, on *Karuna* being the main rasa in Bhavabhuti's own dramas, manifesting itself in various forms. Mirash's own conclusion is representative of the latest position:

    What the verse really means is that in the present play Karuna is the main rasa, but it appears in different forms in different character.

    (*Bhavabhuti*, p. 280)

    But this reveals essentially the same kind of error which Mirashi himself is trying to correct, namely, unwarranted generalisation from a specific reference. In fact, the verse only conveys Tamasa's comment on the events of Act III, events she has witnessed. The reference is to various moods and actions of Rama, Sita, Vasanti, and others in the Act.

43. *Uttararmacharitam*, I.46 (following), II. 26, III 36.

44. See, A.P. Singh, op. cit., pp. 135-163 contain one of the finest critical expositions, after Belvalkar and Dixit, of Bhavabhuti's organisation of various dramatic strands in the play.

CHAPTER 5

Mudra Rakshasam: Poetry and Characterisation

Among the great Sanskrit plays *Mudra Rakshasam* stands out as a unique piece of dramatic composition. Vishakhadatta takes up a purely political story, and with some apparently uninspiring material relating to the world of diplomacy carves out a superb drama. In preparing a play with *Vira* (heroic) for its *angirasa* he selects a minister-protagonist whose principal occupation is to confine himself to his austere cottage and reel off extensive lengths of diplomatic web from its quiet seclusion. There is no sallying forth into fields of martial engagement in the pursuit of honour and glory. *Pratijna Yougandharayanam* of Bhasa, another memorable Sanskrit play with a shrewd, dedicated minister for its main protagonist, furnishes a neat contrast. Yaugandharayana carries himself into the thick of action, infiltrating into enemy kingdom with a bunch of loyal followers and participating in a heroic adventure to rescue his captive king. Chanakya of this play, on the other hand, is almost rooted to the same spot, devising impenetrable strategies, sending out an army of spies and agent provocateurs, constantly brooding over the past and the future, and filling the stage, every now and then, with passionate declamation. The amazing success of his policy should be thrilling material for a story. But to seek to produce an effective theatre-piece out of such material is a daring venture, indeed.

Remarkably enough, Visakhadatta refuses to make use of a romantic sub-plot in the manner of Bhasa to ensure popular appeal. Dramatic interest is rigorously centred on the unfoldment and impact of Chanakya's stratagems. No doubt, events and actions which have been organised are, in themeselves, of an exciting nature. But the focus is always on the intellectual design which has produced these consequences: they are all introduced as 'plotting' and 'fruition' of Chanakya's policy, as one of the verses describes. Delineation of the major events, as such, does not receive much attention, most of the important developments being reported or briefly shown, with the exception of the Chandanadas-Rakshasa episode which features towards the end. For its most part the play is concerned with a mapping of moods and elaboration of intrigues. And, yet, the author manages to create a drama of astonishing theatrical power.

Exhilarating theatricality, indeed, constitutes the major characteristic of *Mudra Rakshasam*. A sophisticated relish of the melodramatic, the theatrical, and the bombastic that we observe, for example, in the Jacobean theatre would have bewildered a Kalidasa. Vishakhadatta, on the other hand, would thoroughly understand and appreciate the approach to drama as primarily theatre, though he would be far from approving the kind of atmosphere, theme and tone that were cultivated by the Jacobean playwrights. It is not as if Vishakhadatta fails to make subtle and complex use of dramatic poetry, or that he ignores the intellectual, moral, or broadly human, problems in order to concentrate on the spectacular. But there is no denying the fact that *Mudra Rakshasam* evinces an extraordinary fascination for the ostentatiously theatrical and rhetorical modes.

Looking at its plot and characterization one finds the play overwhelmingly dominated by one character, namely, Chanakya. In fact, it is difficult to find another character in dramatic literature who envelops an entire play so thoroughly as he. He is the puppet-master manipulating all the strings in the play with a sure and unerring touch. From the moment he enters the stage right at the beginning, he controls the proceedings firmly. Other characters in the play are merely accessories or foils to him. The extraordinary dominance of this character, together with the severely political nature of the subject-matter, creates an impression that the play lacks a broader human interest and that it presents merely intellectually conceived, typical, one-dimensional figures. Secondly, its extroverted rhetorical style gives rise to the supposition that its dramatic poetry has nothing better to offer than fiery bombast and set lamentations. These two questions, which actually emanate from the same dramatic source, constitute the major critical issues in respect of *Mudra Rakshasam*.

Responding to the question of dramatic poetry, we may begin with a study of the introductory verses of the two major, contrasted characters, Chanakya and Rakshasa – apparently, the one sheer bombast, and the other, stylized, conventional lamentation – and observe whether they serve any subtler function than the oratorial. But it would be useful, first of all, to discuss the Introduction proper before looking at Chanakya's verses, for both together discharge the immediate dramatic function of projecting the character in all his massiveness, complexity and power.

The name 'Chanakya' at once evokes feelings of terror and admiration; there is no more awesome minister in all the annals of Indian history. His was a stunning rise to supreme power and fame. Insulted in the court one day by the mighty Mahapadmananda, this learned Brahmin with a quick temper burst out with a vow to decimate the Nandas, and loosened his pigtail as a gesture of his defiance and pledge. Naturally enough, this seemed then a piece of mad arrogance, an outrageous exercise in bombast and histrionics. But within a few years he had performed the incredible feat of reducing the proud Nanda empire to ashes, and installing his protege, Chandragupta, as king. His irascibility, inscrutability, iron-will and ruthlessness acquired a legendary character thereafter. With all this went, however, an utter unselfishness and austerity of character, and a dazzling intellectuality: he has come down to us as the author of the most comprehensive ancient treatise on political economy, *Arthasastra.*

It was, therefore, no easy task to create this character on the stage. Moreover, Visakhadatta's dramatic design made it necessary that it be realised with sufficient power before the initiation of the main action. His masterful use of dramatic poetry can be appreciated from the competence with which he achieves this object. Making a constant and versatile use of paronomasia and *dhvani* (suggestion), resorting to broad, epic similes and metaphors, manipulating a powerful battery of alliterative and assonantal patterns, he produces an unforgettably vivid and penetrating impact by his delineation of Chanakya at the very initial stages of the drama.

The Invocation takes us straight to the heart of the play. Lord Shiva's deft shielding of Ganga against the jealous attention of His consort, Uma, is the theme of the first benedictory verse. Sanskrit commentators have offered a number of interpretations by variously explaining the poetic device employed here.[2] They bring out the significance of the references to Lord Shiva, Ganga and others well enough, but the tenor-vehicle relationship is often misconstrued.

Two of the more popular elucidations compare Ganga and Uma to principles of morality and love, and, in terms of dramatis personae, relate them to Malayaketu and Chandragupta respectively.[3] But, then, there is no conflict between policies of righteousness and love in the play; similarly, the suggested allusion to characters appear to be misconceived because Malayaketu is more antagonistic to Chanakya than to Chandragupta. To start with, the suggestion that the moon as a cover for Ganga stands for Chanakya as a protector of *Dharma*, sounds attractive. His devotion to Chandragupta would in that case be read as a token of his larger interest. But, then, it would be difficult to fit in Parvati to such a scheme of correspondence, because she is hostile to Ganga, and not to the moon. Commentators who draw Malayaketu into the context are similarly wrong. Rakshasa would rather be the more apposite reference: for while he begins by being hostile to the existing political order, later he consents to minister to its welfare. It must be admitted, however, that even this explanation does not fit in with every minute element in the verse.

But, of course, the verse is not designed to secure any such elaborate aptness covering all possible references that might be discovered in it. Its main intension is to exploit the conventional benedictory opening to broadly suggest the main theme of diplomacy; an interesting domestic situation is, therefore, contrived for the supreme Yogi, Lord Shiva, where it becomes necessary for him to resort to a piece of trickery. The choice of Lord Shiva in this context is wonderfully subtle: it establishes a close link with the many facets of Chanakya, who is a learned and devout Brahmin living in austerity, a fierce destroyer of the old state, who adopts a variety of subterfuges and strategems with the sole intention of restoring a healthy political order. There is, again, the unmistakeable suggestion of the tender and charming personality of Chandragupta sustained at his exalted height with the loving support of the mighty Chanakya. The image of the moon-digit[4] (*chandrakala*) perched at the top of Lord Shiva's massive frame, which is besmeared with holy ashes, unerringly captures the personalities of the characters in question, and their mutual relationship: Chanakya's austere, awe-inspiring and benevolent personality serving as a secure cushion to Chandragupta who is essentially a tender, romantic figure.

A far more clear and direct body of suggestions issues from the second verse which describes Lord Shiva performing His tandava dance in a constrained manner. Lest the world should crumble under His mighty pressure, he treads the dancing measure cautiously and gently, and while glancing along all corners of the universal auditorium does not rest His fiery gaze on any particular object for fear it might be reduced to ashes. The obvious points of reference here are the massiveness of Chanakya's personality and his fiery power. A more interesting body of poetic suggestions is thrown up by the phrase, *duhkha nritya*: the uneasy and, therefore, unhappy dance of Lord Shiva beautifully summarises Chanakya's inner state. While piloting his various political moves with marvellous precision and assurance and wielding an unprecedented personal authority, he is still inwardly troubled with the nature of the task which is so much at variance with the basic aspiration he nurses as a learned, self-abnegating, pious Brahmin to remain absorbed in higher intellectual and spiritual pursuits. The picture of Lord Shiva who habitually remains absorbed in a blissful state of meditation, but finds it necessary to perform a *duhkha nritya* for the welfare of the world, neatly captures the quality of Chanakya's mind.

Contrary to the impression he generates with his ruthless and passionate involvement in power-politics, Chanakya is actually pining for a life of quiet seclusion and selfless pieties, as is memorably home out by his concluding act in the play. His restiveness and passion, we then understand, spiring, in some measure at least, from his *duhkha nritya*; but he cannot stop till Rakshasa is won over, and peace and stability are established in the kingdom. The view that the 'uneasy dance' reference to Rakshasa's predicament can hardly find a critical justification. The fierceness of the third eye (by extension, the diplomatic vision, here), the vigour of the *tandava,* the careful survey of the entire arena, would hardly be apposite in respect of the crest-fallen, despairing Rakshasa as it is in the case of Chanakya, whom one of the later verses actually compares to *Rudra* at his *tandava dance.*[5]

The benediction over, the stage-manager now enters to *establish* the plot. The theme and action of the play are comprehensively and engagingly suggested through his 'introductory' remarks. Chanakya's entry is then signalled by a voice from off-stage :

> 'Ah who, whilst I live, dares to overpower Chandra by force'?

On hearing the resounding challenge the stage manager acts taking fright and departs from the stage after hurriedly putting in a few explanatory words which help locate the drama at the particular point of history when Chanakya had just crowned Chandragupta as king after destroying the Nandas through protracted war and diplomacy. The empire is still in the throes of political uncertainty because a number of powerful enemies, among them the redoubtable Rakshasa, are still at large. Brilliantly foiling all machinations of the enemy, and ruthlessly wiping out all opposition, Chanakya has steadily grown in power and stature, but he remains tense and disturbed yet on account of the political situation. Thus his excited rejoinder from off-stage to a portion of the verse spoken by the stage manager – which he misconceives as a threat to Chandragupta.

Soon after the stage-manager departs, the awesome minister strides forward into the middle of the stage and delivers a string of powerful declamations. 'Who dares', Chanakya thunders, 'pluck out its teeth from the yawning mouth of the lion while it lies indolently after tasting an elephant's blood – teeth that are tinted red and look like the digit of the moon at early twilight?'[6] Chandragupta is the feline teeth with which Chanakya has lately pierced and crushed the gigantic Nanda-Elephant. But the qualities of Chandragupta which are more centrally portrayed in the play are his majesty, grace and artistic temperament; hence issues the aptness of the 'moon'-image. A further striking suggestion is contained in the picture of an early moon during the period of twilight which is tinged red like the teeth of the lion after a bloody repast. Chandragupta has only recently completed a bloody engagement, and has just occupied the throne; both he and his kingdom are still in the twilight stage, with his enemies once. again closing in under the leadership of the indefatigable minister of the Nandas, Rakshasa. Some more time has to elapse before Chandragupta can attain to his luminous majesty. When Rakshasa is finally won over, his rule – like the full moon night – would produce a peaceful and soothing atmosphere in the kingdom. Thus, the verse goes to suggest past violence, present phase of transition, and ultimate stage of harmony and peace together. It also neatly projects the fury of Chanakya and the tenderness of Chandragupta.

In his second verse Chanakya points at his black tuft of hair which he had kept untied as a token of his vow of vengeance. 'Who wishes to keep uncoiled (i.e keep his fury unsheathed)', he bellows, 'the hair which was like a black cobra to the Nandas and which is like a line of black smoke rising from some hidden fire?'[7] The terrifying quality of his famous pigtail, its venomous and fiery potential, and the depth of Chanakya's passion are all swiftly conveyed. A reference to the epic quality of his achievement in annihilating the mighty Nandas, backed by the vehemence and sonority of his challenge, and his theatrical gestures, effectively produce the impact of a heroic, awe-inspiring personality.

The third verse[8] reinforces the effect by elaborating the same idea further. 'Who is he', Chanakya exclaims again, 'that is so ignorant of the measure of his own strength and is so much without a sense of discrimination as to risk perishing like a moth by crossing the flame of my wrath – the flame that incinerated the extensive forest of the Nanda-race?' The inexorable sweep of his vengeance and the futility of all opposition against him are effectively conveyed by the straightforward rhetoric of this verse which is kept unencumbered by figurative devices.

These verses illustrate the very essence of Visakhadatta's dramatic poetry; the employment of clear, direct and broad poetic strokes, preference more for similes than metaphors, and metaphors than symbols. But the powerful dramatic context to which this poetry lends its mood and atmosphere, as also the technique of spaced repetition in the use of select images, endow these figures of speech with a potent symbolism, Black tuft of hair and black smoke, in conjunction with bloody mouth and tongues of flame, are simple poetic devices, no doubt. But Visakhadatta's speciality and triumph consists precisely in taking up such simple figures and rendering them surpassingly evocative on the stage. It is dramatic poetry of a supremely effective and precise kind which we enjoy in *Mudra Rakshasam.*

The one who inadvertently occasioned this outburst having already slipped away, Chanakya now calms down on his own, and asks his disciple to bring him a chair. At this point there is a brief, revealing exposure of another aspect of his personality. This colossus whose very presence sent shivers through people and awed the king of the land, now addresses his disciple in a tender, apologetic tone and explains that his occasional brusqueness of manner was only an expression of inward restiveness. Constant preoccupation with political problems made him appear forbidding and severe, and he asks the young neophyte not to take it as an affront. This gentle, considerate, and kindly aspect of his character, so much at variance with his public image, comes as a surprise to the audience. Only later, at the end of the play, when Chanakya's real personality is brought out in its fullness does one realise that the present act of kindly solicitude is very much in character.

Sitting down, he thinks aloud the nature of his present worry. The odds, again, seem insuperably high. But with characteristic audacity and passion he concludes that he would certainly succeed in crushing out all his adversaries. Thoughts of imminent danger provoke him to vehemently affirm his resolution in a series of impassioned outbursts. He declares in a menacing voice that his fury, like a forest-fire, had abated of its own, not because it was exhausted, but on account of the absence of further material to burn. He goes on to declaim how his burning indignation had cast a pall over the bright, moon-like faces of the enemy-women with dark fumes of desolation; the winds of his policy had scattered ashes of stupefaction over the minister-trees of Nanda; and consumed in his fire of vengeance the entire race and following of the Nandas save some 'terror-stricken birds, the citizenry'[9]. He recounts how the arrogant Nanda king who had once spurned him in the court was toppled from his exalted throne as an elephant is sent hurtling down the ridges of a mountain by the ferocious sweep of an enraged lion.[10]

As one examines these introductory verses of Chanakya one is struck by their rhetorical power, dramatic aptness and clear appeal.[11] The declamations create a heroic, charged atmosphere for the play, and introduce its main image of light and darkness. The image deepens the thematic contrast between order and anarchy, reinforces the opposition between Chanakya and Rakshasa, and also introduces the dual aspects of situations and characters in the play which would be amplified, in a Shakespearian manner, through poetic interinanimation. They concentrate on a broad, externalised style in keeping with the theatrical mode of presentation and serve a variety of dramatic purposes such as description of the situation, delineation of the protagonists, and creation of suspense. The entire thing is contrived in an unabashed, rhetorical manner.

The situation demands sententiousness and bombast; while providing these in abundance, Vishakhadatta also succeeds in preserving economy and point with wonderful astuteness. Beside this, much of Tambulaine's mighty lines would appear somewhat shallow, lacking in precision and compactness. An over-profusion of ranting rhetoric at times weakens the appeal of Tambulraine's character. On the other hand, Vishakhadatta's telling concentration on light and darkness through the manipulation of certain broad, well-chosen similes–elephant and lion, smoke and fire, dark jaws and blood-smeared glittering teeth–intensifies the dramatic appeal of Chanakya's fearsome eloquence. While Tamburlaine's prolix perorations continually border on the braggadoccio and cater to an adolescent thrill, Chanakya's concentrated declamation leaves one awed and overwhelmed.

One may now turn to the introductory verses of Rakshasa in Act II to see how they are designed for a powerful piece of dramatic contrast. Rakshasa is the one enemy who is feared and admired by Chanakya, because he combines extraordinary political astuteness with supreme loyalty and dedication to his master. While preparing the audience for Rakshasa's appearance, therefore, Ahitundika is made to say how the goddess of sovereignty was, as it were, left bewildered and undecided by being equally powerfully drawn in contrary directions by the two ministers. He elaborates:[12]

> As the she-elephant moves indecisively, now to one and then to the other of two equally matched, contending tuskers in the forest, so also the goddess of royal fortune appears listless while flitting between the two warring ministers, totally unsure of the ultimate victor.

Such an equally matched state was what the people thought[13] – as also what Chanakya himself believed – existed. The representation of Rakshasa in the verses which follow, however, produces a sharply different impression. Rakshasa's introductory speeches are significant, showing him crestfallen, bitter, and somewhat peevish. It is not that he lacks courage, resolution, or means. But, as he presently describes, all his efforts now lack substance; with the Nanda dynasty totally extinct, championing their cause has become as futile and embarrassing as the efforts of a painter in the absence of a canvas or a wall to paint upon.[14] It is only his profound sense of loyalty which keeps him tethered to the task enjoined upon him by his dead master.[15] Continuing his soliloquy through the next two verses he chides the fickle-hearted goddess of fortune for having so promptly transferred her affection from Nanda to Chandragupta. 'Why did you not', he unpraids, 'vanish at that moment (of Chandragupta's victory) like the line of ichor on the death of the she – elephant?'[16] Deriding her yet more vehemently, he bursts out: 'Moreover, O base-born woman, have all royal persons perished that you selected the low- born Chandragupta as your Lord? Or is the mind of woman naturally unsteady like the tips of *Kasa* flowers, in appreciating the merits of men?'[17]

Constrasted to Chanakya's introductory speeches in Act I, these verses reveal a person who is not just unhappy or agitated on account of misfortune, but one whose emotion is in danger of having the better of him. Chanakya is naturally more full of confidence and aplomb; and the absence of these qualities in Rakshasa at the present moment may only be natural. But what is astonishing is to find the great Rakshasa sunk into a peevish self-pitying mood. Instead of trying to summon his inner reserves to meet the challenge, he gives himself over to a fit of lamentation, and seems to be losing grip on himself. The language he uses to rail at Rajya Laxmi, Goddess of Royal Fortune, shows a certain crustiness which is startlingly incongruous in the context of his grand reputation. While he should be struggling to preserve s solemn determination and severity in his gestures and demeanour, he is laping into a lachrymose, desperate state.

Through the quality of language and tone here Visakhadatta is already indicating the later development of the main action – for, while

Rakshasa is nobly distinguished by his selfless loyalty to a dead master, he is clearly no match to Chanakya in his present state of self – consuming melancholia. The issue will be ultimately decided on the basis of superiority of mental agility and grit. Hearing the laments of Rakshasa one is reminded of the last speech of Chanakya in Act I. However agitated he had seemed through the scene because of Rakshasa's popularity and military strength, at its conclusion he was once again in full possession of his mental resources:

> Those who went (the deserters) by cherishing something in heart have left, indeed; those who still remain may by all means try to run away. May only my intellect, which by itself surpassed a hundred armies in the accomplishment of desired objects and whose great prowess was demonstrated in the destruction of Nanda, may it not desert me.[18]

Rakshasa just cannot command such a supreme self-confidence. His speeches are passionate and lyrical, but they do not have the sonorous vibrancy and majesty of tone that we find in Chanakya's words. More than anything else, the tone and language of their poetry bring home to the spectator the difference between the two protagonists. In other words, Visakhadatta has mastered the art of deploying poetry in creating dramatic atmosphere and character. It is a simple, straight–forward kind of poetry, but one with precise dramatic orientation, and full of significant suggestions. Conventional figures of speech rendered powerfully dramatic through their contextual aptness and subtle overtones, distinguish all these verses. Thus poetry, more than anything else, creates the essentials of drama here, as elsewhere in Sanskrit *natakas*.

An unfailing aptness and rich suggestiveness of poetry engage our attention at every turn in this play. Apart from dexterous use of paronomasia, even simple similes are employed with superb dramatic effect. Sometimes it is an extended simile elaborating upon various strands incorporated into one major object of comparison (as in I.II). Elsewhere, it appears sharing the majesty and power of an epic simile (as in I.8), to impart a heroic dimension to the speaker and to the occasion. But even apparently more circumscribed and simple figures surprise one with their dramatic vividness, clarity and subtle overtones. The last line in 1.12 may be taken as an illustration, conveying the massive stature and exalted eminence of the Nandas together with the extraordinary ferocity and power of Chanakya.

Similarly, in appearance a very ordinary simile in the first half of the next verse – 'the nine Nandas who were like deep darts in the bosom of the Earth were plucked out and the goddess of royalty was firmly established like a lotus in the lake [19] – it is found to contain a wonderfully compact body of dramatic suggestions. While *Samutkhata* (plucked out, uprooted) and *Sthirapada* (with firm feet) are the two contrasted images being described, they are not merely a pair of commonplace opposites. *Samutkhata* suggests severe exertion for uprooting something that is deeply imbedded: here it suggests the great endeavour that had to be made to uproot the hateful Nandas who were firmly established in their sovereignty. The Maurya rule, on the other hand, was a very recent affair. Though not as deeply entrenched as that of the Nandas, and apparently still very shaky, it had already acquired a firm grip on the sub-soil of the empire. The appearance – and – reality equation in this context is neatly suggested with the image of the lotus which constantly sways with the ripples while keeping a secure hold deep down in the mud. The lotus, again, has the traditional mythological support for being the most appropriate object of comparison for the goddess of fortune.

Similarly apt similes are shot through the prose passages, too, with brilliant effect. Dealing with the theme of espionage, contrivance and double–talk, the dialogues are significantly packed with witty double-entendres and oblique references. They also exhibit imaginative excellence of a high order. A quality with which Visakhadatta is usually not credited, namely, sheer creative delight in rendering incidents and situations, manifests every now and then to prove that the playwright is not mechanically engaged in the production of impressive, but made-to-order, rhetorical passages. One might take the example of a prose speech where one would not ordinarily expect a pronouncedly evocative use of language.

While presenting the signet-ring of Rakshasa to Chanakya, Nipunaka the spy gives an elaborate account of the manner in which he came to acquire it. He describes how it slipped from the fingers of a woman and, rebounding on the floor, came rolling down to his feet and remained motionless there, 'like a married girl in the act of bowing to her elders'. Now, the acquisition of this ring is of immense value to Chanakya: he adopts a superb strategy to capture Rakshasa with the aid of this ring (and, hence the title of the play). In the context of this future development the words of Nipunaka acquire a rich measure of dramatic significance. The traditional *kulabadhu* (daughter-in-law of the house) with her bashful, limpid movement, her awe of superiors, her humility and self-consciousness in the act of bowing, makes a charming picture. Against the given dramatic situation this description signifies the ultimate humbling of Rakshasa. *Kulabadhu* suggests a dear and welcome new entrant into the family; so would be Rakshasa won over and kept honoured at the centre of Chandragupta's court.

An interesting point that could be raised here is, if Visakhadatta displays such abundant poetic skill and originality in manipulating conventional figures in a number of complex and suggestive ways, why should he have refrained from incorporating more directly original, creative passages of poetry in the play? That he, too, can introduce superbly evocative poetry when he chooses to, is borne out by the verses describing Autumn in Act III. But he does so very sparingly, only where a significant dramatic purpose is to be served. It is, then, a question of artistic choice rather than one of proficiency. And Visakhadatta's choice is for poetry of a public kind, one which wittily and comprehensively serves the immediate dramatic propose without seeking to attain deeper or more complex poetic results for itself. This may offer relatively a more limited scope to project a profound experience or vision of human life. It may engage the personal emotion of the spectator less intimately and intensely than would a pre-eminently poetic play. And thus Visakhadatta's verse may attain neither Kalidasa's range nor Bhavabhuti's depth. But it achieves greater theatrical immediacy and directness than either because of this very restraint. It is alleged that *Mudra Rakshasam* makes use of too very intricate and pedantic a kind of poetry.[20] But a study of the verses in the play clearly reveals that it is rather the reverse which is true.[21]

Poetry is strictly made subservient to the ends of immediate theatrical response[22] here. What Eliot said of Jonson's verse is largely true of Visakhadatta, too. At one level, it is 'poetry of the surface', and poetry of the surface is, as Eliot said,[23] relatively more difficult to appreciate than poetry of the more directly evocative kind. Just as the apparently unpoetic lines of Jonson reveal on occasion superb dramatic multivalence, so also the conventional poetry of Vishakhadatta offers a rich quarry of dramatic suggestion. Their ends, and hence, the nature of their dramatic poetry are obviously different. But in terms of dramatic irony and suggestion they would bear excellent comparison. Wilson calls Visakhadatta, 'the Massinger of the Hindus'[24],. But neither Massinger nor the more bombastic Marston achieve Visakhadatta's finesse for integration of clarity and complexity throughout a play.

Webster's poetry displays, now and then, the broad, theatrical and yet, subtly complex dramatic strokes which is the pronounced characteristic of Visakhadatta's. But Webster's verse becomes only too often a literary mosaic pressing together a lot of discursive material and joining them up in a laboured style, Visakhadatta is never distracted from his rigorously disciplined pursuit of the immediately dramatic in the interest of witty and complex poetic constructions as happens in Webster. He has chosen a subject that is quite exciting in itself, but of a kind which does not readily lend itself to smooth and easy stage – treatment. And the end in view being the presentation of the more ostentatious *vira rasa*, along with subsidiary elements of terror (*bhayanaka*) and pity (*karuna*), Visakhadatta naturally opts for a heroic, declamatory, 'surfacial' style. The theme demands a poetry which should achieve at the same time clarity and intensity, directness and power, precision and passion. *Mudra Rakshasam* demonstrates how such an objective could be realised through controlled poetic manipulation.

Going into the other question, namely, the quality of its human interest, it may be seen that while the play presents a preponderantly political world and is consequently engaged, for the most part, in projecting the public personalities of its characters, it also offers us closer glimpses of their personal selves. An intimate picture of the private lives and personal reactions of ordinary characters who surround the heroic personalities is carefully inscribed at various points in the play. This is a kind of subtle counterpointing introduced into each Act. In Act I, for instance, Chanakya's colossal personality materialises on a stage that is initially framed for a commonplace domestic setting with its ordinary hubbub and bustle. Before being conducted into the presence of the mighty ones at the centre of the political world, the audience is first of all given a brief, relaxed scene of amusing private conference. Before Chanakya's thundering declamations fill and reverberate through the auditorium they are treated to an interesting assortment of household sounds. The delineation of the great Rakshasa in an isolated state of grief and despair in Act II is, similarly, preceded by the familiar spectacle of a snake – charmer inviting spectators to the show, and is followed by the moving soliloquy of a chamberlaine much advanced in age, reflecting on a constrasted theme – the psychological state of being assailed by bouts of temptation in old age.

Chandragupta's regal entry in Act III is preceded by a brief sequence representing, in ordinary human terms, the private life of his old chamberlaine, Vaihinary. The chamberlaine has grown old in service; at this point of time, not the momentous political issues that envelop his official world, but his own basic human problems are uppermost in his mind. He walks in dejected, musing on his mental unease. His self-pity finds a fuller expression, again, in the middle of the Act. Service, indeed, is misery, he says, and goes on to elaborate:

> First of all, a servant has to be continually in awe of the king; next of his minister; again, of his favourites and, finally, of crafty people who haunt the palace and are in receipt of royal favour.

Soon after, we see Vaihinari going out to convey a message to Chanakya. As he walks on, he muses appreciatively on Chanakya's austere life and the moral basis of the minister's personal authority. Approaching the house of Chanakya he is then shown experiencing a sudden access of fear and awe. Later in the Act, again, the dramatist shows him observing Chandragupta's apparent change in behaviour towards Chanakya and makes him express relief and joy at this development, something that dramatically ushers in matters of interesting personal and political import. All this shows the care Visakhadatta takes in presenting characters as fully and dramatically as possible in the context of the political world he is portraying.

It may be suggested that such lament as Vaihinari voices is rather conventional with chamberlaines in Sanskrit drama, for we come across similar expressions in other plays, as well. Even so, the dramatic impact of the private note, sounded through a representative of ordinary humanity peripherally stationed at centres of political authority, would be no less significant. But, of course, conventional plaints do not sink deep into an audience. Moreover, since the question under discussion is Visakhadatta's special keenness in organising certain private responses and emotions into his political world, if Vaihinari's complaints are in the nature of a casual handling of a stereotype, it would be critically unsound to make it appear specially significant. The atmosphere and tone of his play would certainly inhibit Visakhadatta to an extent; too much of ordinary personal responses are difficult to organise into heroic plays which subserve predominantly political and moral interests. If in spite of this constraint Visakhadatta is found to have attached a more than customary importance to Vaihinari's private meditations and feelings, then, of course, it would be unavoidable to conclude that they serve a special dramatic purpose. And that, precisely, is what comes out if we compare the utterances of vaihinari in this play with those of the chamberlaines in Kalidasa.

The chamberlaine in *Abhijnana-Shakuntalam* has a very brief speech in Act V, in keeping with its intention of incorporating a conventional element:

Ah, for my condition:
This wand, a symbol I once took
As warden of the female court..
How years have sped-it serves me now
But to support my tottering step.[26]

The speech may have interesting dramatic suggestions to offer in the context of Dushyanta's love and authority; it may strike one as both witty and poignant, but in this fleeting, brief aside the personality of the chamberlaine is not being sought to be emphasized. In *Vikramourvasiam* we have Latavya the chamberlaine lamenting his old age in a similar vein. He has, of course, a slightly longer and more elaborate lament, but it is far less impressive than the pithy, dramatic statement in *Abhijnana-Shakuntalam*. In essential terms what is suggested in *Abhijnana* is only elaborately explained there. The chamberlaine in either play ruefully reflects that in the absence of a family to take care of him, he can never look forward to the pleasures of retirement:

All other men when life is green and strong
Marry and toil and get them wealth; then, ageing,
Their sons assume the burden, they towards rest
Their labored faces turn. But us for ever
Service, a keyless dungeon still renewed,
Wears down; and hard that service is which kept
O'er women ward and on their errand runs.[27]

Measured against these so-called 'conventional' interpolations of the chamberlaine, Vaihinari's laments are clearly far more incisive and forceful. He has a much more rounded and effective existence as a character than have Kalidasa's chamberlaines or Bhavabhuti's, though in the case of the latter the original representation in the epic that clearly buttresses the character might help it appear a distinctly developed personality. Vaihinari is far more intimately delineated than the other stock chamberlaines in Sanskrit drama. This, as has already been suggested, is specially significant because the context of Visakhadatta's play would seem to be far less promising for such a close portrayal of an ordinary character and his private problems. Clearly enough, Visakhadatta's more sympathetic and fuller characterisation of this ancillary character involves a definite artistic choice, and not mere conventional grafting.

Such a directly human response concerning one of the supernumerary characters is once again introduced in Act IV, which also begins on a personal note. Kuruvaka the spy comes in with a wry face, and discusses in a soliloquy the inescapable ordeals of royal service before he moves into the higher presence. Act VI, similarly, the most pathetic one in the play, showing Rakshasa at the lowest ebb of his fortune, opens with an unusually free and unconstrained scene of joyous meeting between two friends, Siddharthaka and Samidharthaka. These two would be performing the important function of capturing Rakshasa and bringing to a close the political action of the play, but the scene digresses from this main course to show, first of all, the personal lives of these two private citizens as happy social beings. Irrespective of the tragedy and triumph in the world of eminence, ordinary mortals live out their lives under an altogether different set of compulsions and values, and the main business of the drama takes a pause so that these may find a fuller representation.

In addition, their dialogue serves another important dramatic function–that of projecting a popular view of eminent personalities. As against the picture of social harmony and joy represented through these two characters, the last Act produces in its opening movement a directly antithetical note. The Act, which is filled with sentiments of nobility, self–sacrifice and joy, and which is designed to affirm a harmonious order, opens with two figures of lowly untouchables leading Chandanadas to the gallows. Representing those who carry the burden of the most loathsome tasks in the society; these two advance into the stage, warning men against political perfidy and defiance. This announcement is frequently punctuated by their declaration that people of the higher castes might keep away lest they should be defiled by their touch. Although it would be a historical anachronism to read social satire here, there is no doubt about the 'personal' touch. In the same Act, again, we have the moving private scene of Chandandas and his family before the culminating piece of political high-drama is enacted.

It should be clear, then, that common people and their ordinary feelings and reactions are by design introduced into the play. Some of these provide a fuller perspective on the central political engagement while others are fitted in to produce a broader human appeal. Human interest is sustained by constantly mingling private musings and personal asides with the public acts and speeches of the main protagonists. Reference has already been made to a very brief, but revealing, personal gesture by Chanakya in Act I. In respect of Rakshasa such materials are, of course, incorporated by necessity of the fable (Chandandas episode) as also of his political situation. In the case of Chandragupta, however, there is no immediate dramatic necessity for portraying his deeper personal being. And, yet, Visakhadatta's preoccupation with the specifically human, as against the broadly political, is memorably reflected in the portrayal of Chandragupta.

As against his public image of a ruthless and ambitious person, the first words of Chandragupta in the play evoke an essentially poetic personality, a person with an ingrained romantic disposition who finds royalty rather cumbersome and trying. He begins by expressing his private discontent, and complains that a dutiful king is in permanent bondage. Being constantly watchful of public weal he has, of necessity, to ignore and suppress his personal urges and interests. To add to this, he says, the goddess of royalty, 'like a harlot enjoying ascendence', is hard to please: she shrinks from a stern king in fear of humiliation; does not settle down with a mild mannered one; remains hostile to the foolish, and shies away from the learned; she spurns the timid, and dreads the mighty.[28] The verse is meant not only to suggest, generally, the hard condition of kingship, it is also particularly intended to emphasise Chandragupta's weariness of mind. The next verse in which he expresses his feeling of unease at the impending task of enacting a mock – quarrel with his preceptor reinforces the mood.

Then he ascends the balcony of the Suganda palace, ostensibly to have a full view of the civic decorations made in accordance with his decree to celebrate the famous Autumn festival in contravention of Chanakya's ban – the issue on which the mock- estrangement is to be staged. But, instead of immediately conveying the action to the anticipated sequence of his public expression of disappointment and resentment at the absence of ceremonial preparations, the dramatist shows Chandragupta surveying the wide sweep of an autumnal landscape beyond the city and voicing his rapture and thrill. For the moment the immediate dramatic development is given a pause as, in contrast to his earlier mood of wearines, Chandragupta responds to the immaculate beauty of Autumn with poetic fervour and joy.

These three verses[29] with their sedate tone and mellifluousness produce a pure stream of an inhibited, innocent joy and offer, for the moment, a total transcendence of the violent and complex passions of the political world dominating the play. They carve out an idyllic haven away from the troubled waters of public engagement. A symbolic pressure[30] is gathered out of the picture of peace and serenity they present; the ultimate state towards which Chanakya is laboriously and assiduously piloting the public life would be of such harmony and sweetness. Each of these verses, again, crystallises certain personal qualities of Chandragupta in the mind of the spectator.

Verse 7, a richly evocative piece of lyric, portrays his romantic temperament and poetic spirit which in the context of the Indian dramatic and royal traditions are proper qualities for a monarch of *Dhira-Lalita* type to have. Chandragupta's rule, as underscored by Chanakya in the same Act, is 'minister-controlled'. Like Udayana of Bhasa, his royalty is distinguished by its aesthetic, rather than political dimensions. The second verse beautifully paints selected aspects of the autumnal landscape to furnish morals on propriety, humility and purification. Chandragupta cultivates these virtues in himself, and hence is drawn by these aspects in nature. His self-restraint and humility are dramatically revealed at certain key moments in the play. The verse in question gives it a more directly poetic treatment, and strengthens the image of Chandragupta as more of a poetic personality than a political one, more attractively human than arrogantly royal.

The third verse concentrates on amorous suggestions. Autumn is compared to an adept female intermediary who has brought round the indignant Lady Ganga, so that with the misunderstanding dispelled, she now gracefully moves forward to meet her lover, the Ocean; and thus it is that, as against her turbid and swollen demeanour in the rainy season, now she is said to wear a benign and cheerful look. While this verse highlights once again the romantic, poetic dimension of Chandragupta's personality and indicates his amorous disposition, it also suggests how Chanakya's deft mediation would ultimately prevail, and lead the hostile Rakshasa to a graceful union with Chandragupta. In a final verse which rounds off this movement, Chandragupta shifts his attention from the natural landscape, and comments on the absence of familiar carnival sights (such as, 'amorous gentlemen in pursuit of alluring courtesans with swaying hips'). The description throws light on the contemporary liberal and bohemian aspects of social culture, and, at the same time, reveals the pleasure-seeking, *rasika* character of Chandragupta.

The inner man is, thus, dramatically revealed so as to expand and complement the public personality. In the same manner, Chanakya's personality has been presented both in its public and private aspects in order to delineate character as a rich compound of a number of contrasted qualities. Although he maintains a majestic, forbidding presence evoking fear and awe in everyone, he is essentially a kindly, self-denying and austere person. He extends his tender solicitations not only to the king but also to his adversary Rakshasa, as also to the young neophyte Sarngarava. His arrogance and intolerance are counterbalanced by his generous appreciation of his adversary's merit. It is his courtesy and self-effacing magnanimity, no less than his authority and diplomatic skill, that ultimately overwhelms the noble and mighty Rakshasa. His most unassuming and simple style of living even as he wields incomparable power in the kingdom, as noted by the charmberlaine, indicates his intrinsic moral excellence. The interplay of the public figure and the private self in the character of Chanakya thus constitutes one of the central attractions of the play.

A similar kind of duality and contrast informs almost all the other characters, high and low, to produce a thick dramatic texture. [31] A superficial glance at the sharply constrasted protagonists, Chanakya and Rakshasa, may apparently suggest a somewhat simplistic principle of characterisation and structural organisation. But when one attends to the various strands and overtones that go to portray various characters, and in particular, when one closely examines the functioning of the poetry of the play it becomes possible to realise what a complex mapping of moods and emotions has been achieved by Visakhadatta.

Notes and References

References to the text are from *Mudra Rakshasam*, (Ed.) Jagadish Chandra Misra (Chowkhamba Vidyabhavan, Varanasi, 1972).

1. *Mudra Rakshasam*, V.3.
2. See, Jagadish Chandra Misra, op. cit., p. 5-6:

   "This may be taken as an example of poetic ambiguity. Thus, a variety of *alamkaras* such as *Vyajokti*, *Vakrokti*, *Vyatireka, Utpreksha*, *Apanhuti* etc. are deciphered by critics commenting on this verse. Such situations justify the play of a free critical sensibility in achieving some accuracy of critical explication". The author finds a mixture of *utpreksha* and *apanhuti.*

   Nirupama Vidyalankar in her edition of the play (*Visakhadatta Pranitam Mudra Rakshasam,* Sahitya Bhandar, Subhas Bazar, Meerut, Fifth Edition, 1976) suggests that it is a case of *Vyatireka.*

   R.R. Deshpande (Visakadatta's *Mudra Rakshasam*, The Popular Book Store, Surat, 1948) finds *Vakrokti.*

   Tarinish Jha (*Mudra Rakshasam Natakam*, Ramnarayanlal Veni Prasad, Allahabad, Third Edition, 1978) finds here an example of *Vyajokti*

   M.R.Kale (*Mudra Rakshasam*, Motilal Banarasidass, Delhi, Sixth Edition, 1976) identifies it as Vakrokti.
3. Cf. Jagadish Chandra Misra, op. cit., p.5.

   Kale equates Ganga and Parvati with the sovereignty of Chandragupta and the Nandas respectively (M.R.Kale, op. cit., *Notes*, p. 1). It is difficult to see how this could be explained in the context of Lord Shiva's *protecting* Ganga against Parvati and lovingly permitting each of them a close station beside him. Merely the explanation of "policy" would not be enough. The character equations have to be congruent with the total scheme of the verse.

4. Introduction of an image linked with the moon is specifically prescribed by Bharata for the Nandi (initial benedictory verse) as the moon is the presiding deity of the *rasas*. Here the reference to the moon has a special 'resonance' on account of the name, *Chandragupta*.
5. *Mudra Rakshasam*, III. 30.
6. Ibid., I. 8.
7. Ibid., 1.9.
8. Ibid., I.10
9. Ibid., I.11.
10. Ibid., 1.12.
11. This clear appeal and poetic lucidity in Visakhadatta has come in for praise by Wilson, Keith and others. This aspect constitutes a standard discussion in almost all modern editions of the play.
12. *Mudra Rakshasam*, II. 3.
13. Ibid., II. 2.
14. Ibid., II. 4.
15. Ibid., II. 5.
16. Ibid., II 6.
17. Ibid., II 7.
18. Ibid., I 25.
19. Ibid., 1.13.
20. G.V.Devasthali, *Introduction to the Study of Mudra Rakshasa,* Keshav Bhikaji Dhavale, Bombay, First Impression, 1948, pp. 126-127:

    In prose as well as poetry his is a laboured style, more befitting a scientific than a literary work... His poetry is more artificial still and more difficult, too. This defect he has tried to make up by the width and depth of his scholarship, using a large number of *alamkaras.*
21. R.R.Deshpande is one of the small number of critics who respond to Visakhadatta's poetry with adequate precision (op. cit., p. 15):

    "Visakhadatta had a very fine sense of style. Whether it was prose, or in verse, Visakhadatta knew well which words would suit his purpose best, which combination would be most favourable to the effect intended to be achieved."
22. Critical failure in appreciating the poetry of *Mudra Rakshasam* was fairly common. Thus, we have the following in H.H.Wilson et al.. *The Theatre of the Hindus,*

    Indological Book House, Delhi, p. 93:

    "The author of the *Mudra Rakshasam* was not a poet of the sphere of Bhavabhuti or Kalidasa. His imagination rises not to their level...."
23. Ben Jonson, *Selected Essays*, T.S. Eliot, Faber and Faber, London, Reprinted, 1966.

24. *The Theatre of the Hindus*, op. cit, p. 93.
25. *Mudra Rakshasam*, III. 14.
26. H.W.Wells (ed,). *Six Sanskrit Plays*, Asia Publishing House, Delhi, 1964, p. 243 (Trans. A.H.Edgreen).
27. Ibid., p. 312 (Trans. Aurobindo).
28. *Mudra Rakshasam*, III. 27.
29. Ibid., III. 7.8.9.
30. Ramachandra Shukla is among the small number of Indian critics who appreciatively talk of the poetry in *Mudra Rakshasam*. His comment is perceptive and acute, though somewhat exaggerated. He asserts that, in the interest of drama, Visakhadatta has gone to the extent of making a sacrifice of the poetic imagination. He rightly affirms that no special ideal of style is made to preponderate over dramatic emotions in the play; rather the emotions exert a constant pressure on its style.

    See, Ram Chandra Shukia, *Mudra Rakshasam Natakam*, Ramanarayan Venimadhab, Allahabad, Third Edition, 1976, pp. 12 & 30. But even Shukla does not properly examine the complexity of poetic appeal in *Mudra Rakshasam* and does not argue out the nature of its success. Tarinish Jha points out that Visakhadatta's poetry is conditioned by considerations of dramatic propriety and finds his figures of speech natural and appropriate. But, he, too, does not offer a satisfactory appreciation of this poetry.

    See, Tarinish Jha, op. cit., pp. 42-44.
31. See, LP.Khandelwal, *Samskrita Natya Sahitya*, Vinod Pustak Mandir, Agra, 1976.

    This illustrates the general negligence of critics in bestowing on the play some close scrutiny in order to properly appreciate its success. Some traditional views are only repeated from book to book. Khandelwal, for instance, simply quotes a passage from Keith (p. 26) and believes that with this he has adequately discharged his responsibility as a critic. *Mudra Rakshasam* is usually in the shades – Khandelwal has some eleven pages for the play in his book (pp. 215-226) to forty-seven for *Mrichchakatikam*, and even those eleven pages do not contain much critical discussion.

CHAPTER 6

Urubhangam: Metamorphosis of the Tragic Muse

Urubhangam has found recognition as a tragedy on almost all hands.[1] Critics of Sanskrit drama who affirm an undeviating commitment of this tradition to an optimistic outlook, rendering it entirely inhospitable to the tragic form, find this play somewhat disconcerting, and only grudgingly acknowledge that it is a singular exception, a tragedy. In contrast, a critic like A. B. Keith who tries to project a *Brahmanical* image of the Hindu theatre, and who is unwilling to credit the tradition with potential of the same kind of intensity as the European tragedies,[2] is forced to take a most extraordinary critical position in respect of *Urubhangam.* He submits that its central protagonist is not its hero,[3] and argues that the play cannot be called a tragedy since it portrays the just punishment of an evil person. Keith's, however, is an exceptional stand. By and large, *Urubhangam* has come to be regarded as the lone tragedy in the Classical Sanskrit repertoire.[4] This has such far-reaching significance in respect of the Indian aesthetic tradition and its supporting ethical-metaphysical base, that the subject deserves to be very carefully studied. If it were to be found-thematically and structurally-that the play is, indeed, designed in the manner of a tragedy, then the paucity of tragic plays in the Hindu theatre could be attributed to some later cultural constraints or, as is done by Pusalker,[5] to the pressure of dramatic conventions. The tragic elements incorporated into Bhasa's other plays (as also one entire play, *Karnabharam*[6]) would in that case acquire a special significance and justify a radical reinterpretation of the history of Sanskrit drama as adumbrated in some recent studies.[7]

A proper appreciation of the manner in which Sanskrit playwrights handle tragic themes should very significantly modify our expectations of tragedy both as a source of entertainment and as educative experience. As is known, tragic joy is viewed, both in Western and

Indian criticism, from very widely divergent perspectives. In the West, beginning with Aristotle's formulation of 'its own proper pleasure', namely, 'that of pity and fear', and reaching down to Schopenhauer's idea of tragic *vairagya*, Nietzsche's concept of liberation and Richards' view of harmony of impulses, we have a variety of readings on tragic joy, each quite revealing and persuasive, but only in respect of a few chosen models. And none of these quite describe the experience of Indian 'tragic' plays. *Uttara Ramacharitam* is typical. The happy conclusion of the play, in itself, would not render the epic suffering delineated through Rama and Sita suddenly inconsequential, drowning the entire play's experience in a moment of joyful transformation. What is basic to Bhavabhuti's design is the pervasiveness of the sense of joy even through the most disquieting and distressing moments of the story. It is this feature of the Sanskrit drama which constitutes the major difficulty for the Western critic, for whom the standard forms of tragic handling are illustrated by Greek and Elizabethan tragedies and tragi-comedies.

Hegel's contention that in tragedy there is a conflict not so much between good and evil as between different types of good, while clearly untenable in the context of most Western tragedies, furnishes at one level a correct key to the management of conflict in *Uttara Ramacharitam.* But Hegel's tragic protagonist *violates* some aspect of an eternal order, and is punished; the play rehabilitates the order, and hence issue peace and joy. The protagonist in the Sanskrit play might appear to be violating some order, but, in reality, he is not guilty of any such transgression. Whatever cruel or undesirable acts he might perform they would all be in accordance with, all in the service of, order – a sacrifice, and not a transgression. Again, since the order would not be disturbed in the Hegelian sense, its joyous reestablishment would not constitute tragic joy in Sanskrit *nataka.*

When one turns to Sanskrit aestheticians and commentators, one finds a similar lack of unanimity in regard to the question of joy in tragic drama. While some like Ramachandra – Gunachndra emphasize a strict division of plays into joyous and painful ones, Abhinavagupta suggests that, though the rasas (except for *Santa)* combine elements both of joy and grief, they are all 'sukhapradhana'. To Abhinavagupta, the human mind is so organised that it always admits of a paradoxical union of contrary impulses. Apprehension of reversal at moments of joy is as natural a reaction as hope of alleviation in moments of despondency and grief. But all such dualities vanish in the relish of *rasa*; the mind becomes 'ekaghana', totally absorbed, and in a state of 'visranti' or rest, allows the self to experience *ananda.* Sanskrit canonists offer their favourite example of a dish, or a glass of sherbet, in which sweet and bitter ingredients combine to produce a special deliciousness. Some of the arguments are akin to those advanced by European theoreticians. Dhanika, for instance, differentiates grief in real life from its aesthetic realisation where the emotion becomes supremely relishable. Bhattanayaka's seminal discussion on 'Sadharanikarana' in art is directed at showing how *karuna* (that is, tragic material in general) is divested of the potency of personal agony through the process of universalisation and how a sense of joy and relaxation descends into the mind of the spectator with his absorption in the life of the dramatised character and consequent transcendence of personal coordinates.

From Abhinava to Viswanatha there is also to be found dissemination of another, essentially Hindu view of tragedy, or of literature in general, which emphasizes the supra-mundane nature of *rasa*, one that transcends ordinary concept of cause and effect, and is ultimately intelligible as 'brahmananda sahodara' – akin to divine bliss. This is not to be mis-read as a dissociation from reality. The concept of divine bliss as being illustrative of aesthetic joy only seeks to emphasize its non-utilitarian, impersonal quality. And, hence, whether it is a story of grief or of joy that is being dramatised, it is finally immaterial in this sense, for in either case the spectator is rendered oblivious of his ordinary personal emotions, and raised to a highly refined state of perception. As he transcends the social self or ego, and gets established in the deeper substratum of his perennial self – which, according to Hindu philosophy, is constituted of pure joy – he enjoys that divine state of Being naturally and spontaneously. Drama is only a medium to rouse him into an elevated mood, and propel him beyond the realm of custom which has settled upon his psyche, "heavy as frost, and deep almost as life", so that he is once again in tune with his immortal, all-joyous self. From Ramachandra-Gunachandra's emphasis on theatrical 'Camatkara' (thrilling, marvellous spectacle of drama), or Bhojaraja's sexual illustration of joy-in-pain, or the purely psychological theory of *rasa*, to the mystical-philosophical suggestions of divine joy, Sanskrit aesthetes have covered a vast and various territory in their efforts at defining tragic joy.

Keeping in mind these various positions in Indian and Western aesthetics, but seeking to vindicate none of them in particular, one ought to study the texts with an open, informed mind and try to understand how, repeatedly tackling themes and situations that are pronouncedly tragic in character, Sanskrit drama never, in fact, built what the West thought was the proper tragic experience. *Urubhangam* of Bhasa, representing the earliest phase of Sanskrit dramatic tradition known to us, is particularly relevant, indicating the growth of a typical Indian approach to tragedy long before the aesthetic tradition had congealed into standard shapes. We may now turn to the play.

Urubhangam dramatises the events of the final day's battle in the great Mahabharata-war. Millions of warriors who had assembled to fight the epochal war at Kurukshetra have by now perished. Only a handful of the chief contenders, and some stray soldiers, are left alive. The one who was principally responsible for this terrible carnage, Duryodhana, now stands alone, bereft of his legions, his famed generals, and his ninety-nine valiant brothers. The play deals with the final encounter with the redoubtable Pandava prince Bhima whom he is going to meet in single combat. Bhasa uses the form of a long one-Acter in order to portray this climactic phase. He manipulates a kind of pyramidal structure, designing the play to embrace a large thematic base while converging upon a sharply pointed dramatic experience. In order to produce, within a small compass, this impression of large perspective steadily narrowing down to concentrated, illumined focus, Bhasa begins by making a brilliant and novel use of *Sthapana.* He has always been versatile and extraordinarily innovative in organising dramatic introduction[8], but the *Sthapana* and *Viskambhaka* in this play are handled with especial finesses and elegance.

The play opens with the traditional *Sutradhara* (initiator) advancing in to the fore-stage, but in the company of a male attendant, and not his mistress, as is the usual practice.[9] These two bear the burden of properly *establishing* the culminating dramatic moment against the background of the epochal war which has been fought through the past seventeen days. In a very effective piece of choreography, they project a terrible scene of death and desolation surrounding them and offer succinct choral comments on various aspects of the battle. Two main aspects of the war are emphasized: one of glorious 'dharma', righteousness and sacred duty; and the other, of evil propensities and colossal devastation. It was not, after all, an ordinary war. More than any other war experienced or visualised by men it was a war to end all wars – the apocalypse at the end of a *yuga.* It began, as all wars do, with the evil machinations of a small coterie and spread like a forest conflagration, engulfing an entire civilization. But it was also considered a holy war, ordained by divine plan to occur at the transitional period between the epochs of Dvapara and Kali. Even kings who were neutral to both the hostile factions eagerly came forward to participate in the battle, for death on this battle-field was looked upon as liberating. Thus, the war involved two dimensions: one, of evil self-aggrandisement, and the other, of sacred duty.

The two detached commentators begin the drama by projecting both these aspects through subtle and evocative descriptions. They paint all the gory details of the battle-field and also project images of beauty. Beginning with a wide survey of the landscape against the four quarters, and then describing all the gigantic and tiny objects strewn over the field of blood, these 'inducers' lead the audience engagingly, by stages, to the focal point of the drama, the famous mace-fight between Duryadhana and Bhima. The comprehensiveness of evocation and the dexterous tapering off towards the central event are achieved with economy and power. At the same time as a powerfully realistic and moving account of the war is offered, the audience is kept aesthetically distanced by means of elaborate and subtle poeticisation of details. Much as the initial description of the battle has two contrasted aspects, the play proper concentrates on two major, contrasted elements in the mind of the protagonist-agony and ecstasy, passion and calm. But in order that the spectator may properly respond to such a paradoxical integration of opposed moods through the entire length of the play, both an experience of deep emotion and a certain aesthetic detachment in relation to the dramatic situation are to be infused into his mind from the very beginning. The introductory movement is designed precisely to this end.

In a more directly organic Induction (the *Viskambhaka*), thereafter, three ordinary soldiers are introduced: they are non-combatants, enjoying a status midway between direct participants and neutral onlookers, a status which is dramatically significant in the context of the job they are called upon to perform. They, too, begin by describing the scene of horror and desolation, and function as a choral trio offering searching comments on events past and present. They help intensify feelings of horror and grandeur in the minds of the audience. While keeping the attention of spectators concentrated on the very same objects, Bhasa conveys them from one set of emotions to another with remarkable virtuosity.

Their first words emphasise a poignant confrontation: 'We are here; these are here, too' (*these* referring to the dead bodies of fellow-soldiers). After the cryptic observation, one of them sums up the scene:

> Here is the land of enmity, which served as a touchstone for might; the field of fame and distinction; a 'swayambara' – court for heavenly dames; an institution for consecrating men's valour; a proper, martial bed for kings in their last hour; an *agnihotra yajna* for offering the libation of life: we have arrived at the hermitage named war.

In place of the dust and sweat, the fury and agony of a battle-field we have here a picture covering an extended body of evocations from 'the land of enmity' to 'hermitage'. The second one offers a more poignant physical picture comprising feelings of both fascination and revulsion: the field, full of carcasses of elephants, turned into a colony of vultures, the chariots empty and still after the Lords of the earth have moved to heavenly worlds, and so on. The third soldier then provides a closer view of the waste and desolation, but he, too, uses the details to work up an elaborate simile of a *yajna*, introducing thereby implications of religious possibilities.

The bi-polar attitude thus established, a series of five verses are reeled off by the soldiers in quick succession leading the sense of horror and waste to a climax. But once again there is a return to the former mood in Verse 12 which compares the battle-field in the sun, covered with the dead bodies of caparisoned beasts and brightly clad warrior-kings with their dazzling armour, to 'the star-studded firmament which seems to have crashed on the earth'. Interestingly, these very same objects of description in the previous verses had been used to produce a gory, terrifying impact. The transition in mood is now absolutely clear:

> Oh, how bright the warriors look even in death: with the upturned, radiant faces of the dead kings the battle-field looks like a vast, breezeless expanse of lotus-filled earth. Their sagging eye-balls look like bees, the lips suggest tender red leaves, eye-brows suggest the filament of flowers....

After the feelings of revulsion and fascination, of waste and achievement, are thus established in the mind of the audience, the playwright ushers in the main dramatic event. The progress of the mace-fight between Duryodhana and Bhima is then vividly described by the choric commentators who also tellingly capture the reactions engendered by different stages of the fight in the onlookers-Valarama, Krishna, Vyasa, and the Pandava brothers. In a delightfully cinematographic fashion the total situation of the war leading upto the crucial mace – fight is thus impressed in the mind of the audience. The choric voices describe how Duryodhana's agility and superior training bring him an early victory. But he is trounced soon after: Bhima resorts to a course of attack proscribed in the rules of mace-fight, and breaks the thigh of an unwary Duryadhana. The play proper, *Urubhagam* (the Broken Thigh), now begins.

With Duryadhana fallen and lying abjectly sprawled out on the ground with a broken thigh, action of a dynamic kind which kept everyone vigorously engaged through the past seventeen days now comes to an end. The hour of contemplation and reflection has come. Through a superb dramatic design, Bhasa prepares his play as a compact psychological, reflective piece. All that now happens, all the characters who are now introduced on the stage and all their diverse reactions to the pathetic sight of the redoubtable warrior lying incapacitated and forlorn have a single, precise orientation: illumination of the inner world of the protagonist. Interiorisation of dramatic action is thus achieved by the introductory movement which streamlines all preparatory material to sharply converge upon the mind of the hero. Duryadhana's physical immobility is dramatically exploited to intensify the concentration on his mind. Thus, there are two main points to be noted in respect of the initial movement of the play-one, the playwright wishes to emphasize both noble and vicious aspects of the epic action culminating in the protagonist's fall, and, second, the dramatic focus on the mental state of the protagonist at his dying hour.

The situation makes for a highly sensational opening; the prevailing background of deathly silence, the proud hero lying supine on the ground in an agonised state, and the figure of an outraged Valarama, the mighty Yadava elder of Sri Krishna, looming behind. A few moments after this eerie tableau sinks in the mind of the spectator, Valarama advances upon the stage. The earlier fury and violence in his bearing is now softened, and his countenance is wreathed in sorrow. Slowly and mediatively he treads upon the forepart of the stage and muses on the pathetic state of his beloved disciple. He compares Duryadhana to Vasuki[10] at the end of the churning of the ocean of milk – an apt comparison, suggesting the epic quality of Duryodhana's struggle, his essential majesty, and his present state of exhaustion and agony. It also achieves a deeper appropriateness of poetic evocation, bringing to the mind one of the consequences of Duryodhana's protracted struggle: much as the churning of the ocean had produced both nectar and poison, so also the epochal war set in motion by Duryadhana has been an instrument of agony and liberation, both individually and collectively.

The contrast between Duryodhana's earlier state of royal splendour and authority, and the present one of abject misery and helpnessness, provides the background for a deeper contrast between his earlier disposition of egotism, selfishness and vindictiveness, and the present one of humility, clarity and magnanimity. When his mighty preceptor thunders out a portentous threat that Bhima may not yet be allowed to get away with his ill-gotten prize of war, Duryodhana, instead of expressing gratification, is anxious to prevent Valarama from doing harm to his erstwhile enemies. It provides a strangely moving experience to the audience to see the incorrigibly belligerent Duryodhana now pleading for peace and forebearance.[11] Undergoing terrible physical agony, he has still achieved at this final hour of his life a superior perspective on reality, and, hence, for the first time in his career now speaks words of wisdom and pacifism.

Nothing, hereafter, can blur the clarity of his new-found vision, or deter the nobility of his spirit. Even the fact of his being defeated through the adoption of a mean, dishonest trick by Bhima does not generate in him feelings of outrage or vendetta; rather, he seeks to express a measure of gratification in that, even in his fall, he has proved himself truly unconquerable. 'I am not vanquished, then', he declares contentedly, and argues with Valarama that the spirit of anger and vindictiveness had now become utterly meaningless, because most of the personalities who constituted the main counters in the just concluded game of war were now no more. Further hostilities would be utterly purposeless, insane acts. When Valarama iterates in great fury that Bhima should not, in any case, be allowed to enjoy an undeserved victory, Duryodhana calmly rejoins he has been overpowered, not by Bhima but Lord Krishna Himself,[12] and with that silences Valarama. It is needless to mention that his answer marks a profound understanding.

Clearly, Duryadhana's longing for peace is founded upon deeper reasons than the one he advances in the beginning, namely, futility of further fight in the absence of the main contenders. Over and above such pragmatic considerations, there is a firmer ethical commitment reflected in his present pacifist outlook. The other arguments he advances to absolve Bhima of all blame, and the tenacious efforts he makes to persuade Valarama (and later, Aswatthama) against further hostilities, reveals a new-grown faith in values of peace and forgiveness. This, in the context of his earlier personality, amounts to a supreme moral triumph. At the moment of his greatest reversal, humiliation, and suffering, therefore, he has come out victorious, and has achieved a wonderful inner metamorphosis. Instead of falling a prey to natural feelings of grief, indignation, jealousy and despair, he accomplishes a dazzling moral transcendence and even while undergoing excruciating physical pain, achieves peace within himself and with all the world. As the protagonist enacts on the stage such a paradoxical state of agony and ecstasy, the audience is made to experience a feeling of moral elevation. The sensational opening, therefore, functions in an un-Jacobean fashion, intensifying serenity rather than terror, ushering in a religious sense of harmony and acceptance rather than a morbid psychological state of loathing and grief.

Having established in the mind of the audience a new image of Duryodhana–different from what was there in the original story– Bhasa now goes forward to centre dramatic interest on an extended delineation of pathos. The extraordinary fortitude and mental strength Duryadhana has preserved through his present distress is now exposed to a battery of overpowering emotional assaults. Introducing now the shrunken reminder of his family, Bhasa presents, in succession, Duryodhana with his child, with his blind parents, and with his two wives, and works upon this simple design to produce an unforgettably compelling sequence of pity and sorrow. The situation remains the same all through; but, according as the personalities change dramatic emotion is worked out in varying styles and degrees. It is the same emotion of pathos that is built up and amplified over a long stretch, but the playwright manages to furnish an engaging variety, and to build up keen dramatic interest on this rather stereotyped and circumscribed theme. It would appear, then, in spite of Duryodhana's moral and psychological elevation, the play as a whole is designed to be intensely poignant and pathetic. In that case, the nobility of the protagonist, coupled with a moving delineation of his physical suffering and mental distress leading to death, would produce in the audience a deeply tragic experience. We may, therefore, closely examine the sequence-something that does not find mention in the Mahabharata–in order to ascertain its orientation and impact.

Dhrutarastra, the blind Kuru patriarch, enters in the company of his wife, Queen Gandhari, his two daughters-in-law, and his only surviving grandchild, Durjaya. Groping his way through the battle-field, he goes on calling out piteously for his fallen son. 'Having fathered a hundred robust and valiant sons, am I no longer to remain worthy of receiving oblation even once after my death?' he laments in bitter anguish. Gandhari's state is even more sorrowful. As Valarama comments in a voice charged with admiration and pity,[13] she has kept herself blindfolded ever since her marriage, determined not to enjoy a comfort fate has denied her husband, and even at this extreme juncture would not violate her pledge. Experiencing all the bitter pangs of a mother's heart, and yet heroically suppressing an irresistible longing to look at her wounded son, she keeps the covers on her eyes and, like her husband, gropes about in search of the fallen Duryodhana in the desolate field. The lament of his venerable old parents pierces the heart of the dying hero who remains suspended in a state of speechless agony. When he sees his royal queens moving through the field of battle, tearful and forlon, he can bear it no more:[14]

> I could ignore the pain produced by the wounds inflicted by the mace of Bhima, but now that I see my queens moving about with dishevelled hair, the pain is searing and overpowering.

Lest he should break down under the pressure of emotion, he does not at first respond to the call of his parents and, seeing but unseen, lies in obdurate silence. The words of address used by Dhrutarastra at this time – 'crown – gem of my race', 'king of eighteen legions' etc. – are weighted with dramatic irony. Although Dhrutarastra makes use of the expressions with a certain degree of conscious pride, and attempts to buttress the drooping spirit of his son, he known only too well that he is trying to zealously evoke a past whose extinction is all-too-pathetically evident. And so his broken spirit can hardly hold out any longer, and he finds it impossible to sustain the artificially cultivated tone of majesty. Discarding all ceremonial forms of address, then he calls out in a quivering voice – 'O, the eldest of my hundred sons (and the last one to be dying)'.

Duryodhana now finds it hard to restrain himself. In a choking voice he mutters an apology and says grief and embarrassment at meeting them in his present state had forced him into silence. Dhrutarastra, of course, hasn't heard, but it is easy for him to guess the mental state of Duryodhana, and he calls upon his son to greet with his usual cheer and majesty and to be thoroughly contemptuous of the so-called defeat, In a spurt of emotional excitement Duryadhana attempts to rise and move forward to greet his parents, oblivious for the moment of his broken thighs. The very next moment he collapses on the ground with excruciating pain – 'Ah, here is the second hit', he wails out painfully, and then pathetically laments:

> Bhima has not merely plucked my hair and shattered my thighs with his mace, he has also robbed me of my ability to pay respect to my elders.

This verse movingly expresses Duryodhana's grief on being made an exile from the world of regard and courtesy. It is not only that people will no more show him the regard appropriate to his royalty; he himself, too, cannot participate in civility even from the offering end. Failure and deprivation in respect of the most important formal element in the world of royalty brings home to him the real extent of his humiliation and defeat.

One may now witness his earlier sense of exaltation and moral clarity being gradually eroded by an upsurge of sentimentality. A series of encounters and exchanges follow, swelling the tide of sentiment and passion. When he sees his young son Durjaya (not mentioned in the original) tugging at the clothes of the revered, monarch and leading him on, his grief and embarrassment deepen to an extreme degree. He hears his son complaining of exhaustion while his old father coaxes the boy to scout round a little longer. He hears Dhrutarastra encouraging Durjaya and saying, if he strove a little more he can rest on the place dearest to him, namely, the laps of his father. The short scene which then follows raises the pathos to a climax.

When Durjaya manages to reach the spot and finds Duryodhana supine, he stands petrified with astonishment and exclaims to himself, 'Oh, the king my father is resting on the bare ground !' Holding his emotions in check and striking a casual tone, Duryodhana asks him, 'Son, why do you come here?' Durjaya merely repeats in all innocence what his elders had earlier told him – 'Because you have delayed your return'. As Duryodhana keeps musing how even in his present state he was still hungering for the loving caress of his son, Durjaya blithely moves forward and settles down on his thigh. Duryodhana cries out in agony and roughly pushes him away. Immediately after, he bewails[15].

> Alas, that moon-like one who was a veritable feast to these eyes, who caused this heart to dance in ecstasy, the very same moon has been transformed by time and experience today into a burning flame.

Piqued and wide-eyed, the child demands uncomprehendingly, 'Why do you prevent me from sitting on your laps today?' In deep distress Duryodhana can only murmur, 'Son, give up from today your old favourite seat. Try to find some other place to sit around here. This (my lap) is no longer fit for your purpose'. Hardly a more eloquent dramatic suggestion could have been provided to convey that the princeling has now to fend for himself, and find some new shelter. As this thought keeps rankling in Duryodhana's heart, in his innocence Durjaya insists that he would not go in search of some other place, but would 'follow' his father. With a heavy load of melancholy and bitter irony in his tone, Duryodhana rejoins hoarsely: 'Go, son, and tell this to Bhima' (the one who had killed all his uncles and given the deathblow to his father).

The despair and grief gripping the heart of Duryodhana at this point need no further elaboration. Bhasa, therefore, ends the dialogue between father and son without any histrionics or loud laments. The sequence is an example of the concentration of effect Bhasa achieves in his plays *dramatically* rather than through description or sentential, an achievement that often goes unrecognised by critics with a taste for the ornate.[16] Indeed, there are only a few scenes in world drama which may claim to surpass this brief episode in terms of pure dramatic pathos. With this sequence, then, it would seem the initial focus on moral-psychological exaltation of the protagonist was only designed to darken his present despondency. But, in fact, this is organised as a transitional movement. The depth of suffering, despair and bitterness of the protagonist is projected here only to brilliantly set off the resurgence of moral faith and mental exhilaration which is to follow soon after. There would be two main directions to the dramatic emotion now – intensification of pathos through dramatisation of sorrow of the old couple and the queens, and gradual recrudescence of the original mood of contentment and faith in the protagonist. For the audience, therefore, there would be an extended exposure to emotions of sorrow and exaltation concurrently.

Dhrutarastra, Gandhari, and the queens approach Duryodhana. Dhrutarastra laments aloud that his son, who was a radiant pillar of strength, is now 'transformed into as inert a thing as the nether half of the hinge fitted to the main gate of the palace, and an illustrious king, lay on the ground today like a person (who had renounced the world and was) practising penance and self-mortification' (verse 45). While he expresses his anguish in such moving verses pregnant with a rich body of poetic suggestions his brave consort Gandhari comes forward displaying exemplary understanding and self-possession. She approaches her son with the same supreme composure that has characterised her entire life. She knows fully well how deeply agitated and embarrassed the haughty, fallen warrior must be feeling. She is not going to permit herself an unrestrained abandon in grief; she would consult, not her own emotion, but that of her son. She must bring to him whatever psychological relief is possible and this can be done only by exhibiting heroic self-control in herself.

She preserves a level tone, and taking advantage of her blind-folded state and pretending that Duryodhana's injury is nothing very fatal, she behaves as if she thought he was only resting there, and calmly asks, 'Are you fatigued, child?' But, then, Duryodhana understands his mother only too well. He knows with what supreme self- restraint a heroic mother was seeking to keep her suffering to herself and trying to assuage the psychological distress of her child taking recourse to play-acting. He is overwhelmed by the tender, yet heroic, gesture, and replies with a measure of pride and self-gratification, 'I am, indeed, your child'. Much as Gandhari does not allude to the debacle and says something ordinary to ease the tension so also he ignores his own suffering and seeks to alleviate her grief by expressing his tender regard for her, and his feeling of pride on her account.

Sensing someone coming close to him Dhrutarastra now asks, 'Who is there?' And Gandhari promptly answers – 'Lord, I am Gandhari, the famed mother of fearless children'. The orientation of her answer is obvious. Subtly, patiently, and heroically, she is taking every bit of opportunity to instil courage into the mind of her dying son. What must be the most unbearable pain for Duryodhana at this moment, she well knows, is the gall of defeat. She sets about valiantly, therefore, to buttress his spirit. And she does it in an unostentatious manner, the only way it can be soothing and acceptable to the fallen warrior. One can easily see the impact of her words on Duryodhana; for, now he is found to be already recovering his original balance and grip over himself. His recently acquired clarity of vision and moral exaltation now return, and he gratefully comments: 'I feel as if today I am born anew'. As may be seen, the pattern of psychological drama behind apparently simple statements and situations is the most outstanding quality of Bhasa's dramatic style.

This is the supreme moment of transition in the drama. Whatever feelings of loss, disappointment and bitterness had suddenly erupted in the mind of the protagonist on account of an overpowering emotional upsurge are now thoroughly cleansed, and he recovers his feeling of elation and clear sightedness once again. This clear sightedness is not of the nature of a sudden 'tomorrow, and tomorrow, and tomorrow' as in Macbeth nor is the elation a matter for 'heroic' declarations appropriate for an Antony. At one level, it is certainly that; for Duryodhana has developed both a sense of futility about his old ambitious, militant ways, and a sense of pride on having gone forward to meet his end heroically. That is the burden of the next two verses, which he utters in a tone of vibrant defiance. With a mighty accession of will-power and pride, coupled with tender solicitude for his parents' mental peace, he begins by appealing to his father to develop a proper 'kshatriya' perspective on the prevailing situation:[17]

> Father, do me the favour, I pray, of giving up your grief by considering that I have been wounded while fighting valiantly in the presence of all. This your proud son, who bent only at thine feet, is journeying forth today into Heaven, thoroughly contemptuous of the leaping flames (on the pier), maintaining unsullied the same honour and nobility he was born with.

Duryodhana's valour–as Vyasa, too, narrates–is going to earn him heavenly reward. This confidence in an otherworldly compensation effects a fundamental kind of change in the so-called 'tragic' elements of loss and futility in the play. Both the constrasted aspects of the war, so elaborately pictured form the beginning, now receive an integrated dramatic representation. Duryodhana's address to his queens emphasizes this fusion of martial glory and righteous fulfillment. To one of them he appeals with a stirring martial gesture. He shows her his wounds, which are all there on the fore-part of his body, and says, 'O soldier's spouse, even when you see that your husband has not been killed in flight (but in courageous encounter), why do you grieve?.[18] To his other wife he talks in a different tone, pointing out the happy aspects of the life he lived, his satisfactory performance of not only political and martial obligations, but also social, domestic, and individual acts of piety and service[19]. Thus, his emotion at the moment is compounded of strains of martial elation and moral satisfaction. His confidence in a higher kind of fulfillment in the other world and his moral faith are also diversely suggested by the playwright at a number of points during the sequence.

His parting words to his mother, in contrast, are altogether in a different key. Himself heroic, he well understands the heroic personality of his mother and is also certain that she understands his feelings perfectly well. There is, therefore, no need for him to offer any exhortation or explanation. He simply speaks a few pithy, moving words of farewell to her – 'I salute you, revered mother, and, on the strength of whatever pieties I have earned through this life I pray (God) that I may again have you as my mother in my next birth'. Gandhari then rejoins in a cryptic style, 'You have but spoken out my heart's desire'.

Finally, he calls Durjaya to his side. As he does so, both his parents suddenly become tense, and whisper to each other in an agitated manner–what parting counsel would he deliver his son? Any sensitive spectator would at once understand the implication of the anxiety evinced by the old couple at this juncture. The unspoken question which hammers in their minds and in the mind of the spectator is, whether Duryodhana, whoever was an unforgiving, haughty person, would at this final hour pass on to his young son an inheritance of the old dynastic feud and enjoin upon him a duty of vendetta (a thing that would be binding on Durjaya) and, thereby, perpetuate the misery of the Kuru clan, or on the contrary, offer the child a more wholesome advice.

The suspense is soon resolved. True to his newly-acquired elevation, nobly transcending his life-long passion of hatred and hostility against the Pandavas, Duryodhana solemnly instructs Durjaya to show his Pandava – cousins the same regard that he would pay his parents. He also exhorts his son to eschew feelings of bereavement and depression after his death by remembering that he had been killed in a martial prowess. In a moving tone he then goes on to picture a future scene: 'After my death, while bathing in the company of my Pandava brothers, holding on to Yudhisthira's mighty arms covered with silken clothes, offer thou some oblation in my name'[20]. This provides a deeply moving, yet controlled, expression to a complex body of feelings and emotions, and constitutes a culmination of Duryodhana's human sentiments, moral courage, and clear sightedness.

The picture of a future after his death that he envisions here operates in a number of ways. The verse, it may be noted, is the concluding one in a sequence where Duryodhana's emotions as a member of his family are being delineated. That is how the reference gains an interesting emotional and tonal multivalence. At the same time as it projects Duryodhana's final victory over his lower self, his transcendence of past animosities and rivalries, a certain undertone of regret and disappointment – even, envy-is rendered quite plain. That is the force of the image of Durjaya gripping Yudhisthira's 'mighty', silk–covered arms, while offering oblations in the river. A soft note of sadness – not bitterness, though – clearly persists, and renders the scene compellingly human. The point is underscored by the comment of Valarama which then follows: *Aho Vairam Paschattapam Samvrttah* (Oh, the mood of hostility has now changed into one of nostalgia and regret).

It is important to understand the nature of Duryodhana's mental state at this climactic moment in the central sequence of the play. In the face of distressful situation he has saved himself from precipitately sinking into despair and bitterness, and has succeeded in regaining the emotional balance he demonstrated in the beginning of the play. He has achieved a triumphant victory over his former self–its moral confusion and egotisical passions. But at the same time he remains movingly human. While delineating his moral growth, the dramatist is careful to see that it is not rendered unnatural, with all normal human sentiments drained out. A certain balance between moral transcendence and emotional mooring imparts to the play an extraordinary charm, and to the protagonist a superb dramatic appeal.

We shall find again a similar interplay between moral self-transcendence and human sentiments at the final moment of his death. At its conclusion, too, the play seeks to project Duryodhana as an extraordinary being, transformed by virtue of his newly acquired sensibility, but not by smothering out the ordinary human susceptibilities and emotions in his character. He is not, that is to say, a simple morality figure lending himself to a sudden, mechanical transformation. His royal sentiments and personal emotions abide till the very last, his feelings as a human being continue to surface in a variety of ways – poignantly, arrestingly – and yet, his victory over self is not for once suspected to be fleeting or contrived.

Such a balance, we all know, is essential in the context of the higher tragic form. But, whether it is to that end that the playwright has designed the play's action can be ascertained only after examining the concluding episode of the play, which now begins with Aswatthama's advent on the stage.

Aswatthama's portrayal initiates a movement that is prepared once again to throw into relief Duryodhana's moral earnestness. One of the greatest among Duryodhana's generals, Aswatthama was away observing the funeral rites of his father, the reverend preceptor Drona, who had been killed by the Pandavas through the adoption of a devious trick. Aswatthama has, therefore, returned with an intense longing for revenge. Before he arrives on the stage, Valarama – in his by now established choric function – offers a description, first, of the twang of his fearful bow, and second, of his personality, based on the 'raudra' and 'vira' rasas respectively. Aswatthama strides in furiously, stamps about the stage, and intensifies the terror- inspiring qualities of heroic indignation already referred to, by means of a series of declamatory verses.

He declares, he has arrived at the end of a *Yajna* to perform the concluding rites – an image, we remember, that had been iterated and amplified by means of elaborate similes in the introductory movement of the play, and one that is apt for a Brahmin – warrior. As did the *Sthapana*, Aswatthama's words, too, take us back to the beginning of the Mahabharata–war. But Aswatthama does not merely remind us of the earlier events – more importantly, he also affirms a continuation of the old mood by pointedly announcing that he is re-entering the field 'with the very same spirit' that was there in him at the time of his first entry[21] (verse 55). He is determined not to concede that it has now become irrelevant and pointless. He is not able, or willing, to appreciate the fact that, together with Duryodhana, the earlier passions are in their dying embers. He wishes to revive the old belligerency in Duryodhana, and so his passionate outbursts before the dying leader are ineptly pitched on a high key of heroics[22] (verse 57, along with the prose dialogues). The audience, however, understand the ineptitude; but also experience some tension as they know what is to follow. Aswatthama has in him the capacity for wreaking devastation of the kind he promises, and because of the background against which he makes it, his bombast is sickening.

Aswatthama repeats the strains earlier struck by Valarama, namely, that the great Duryodhana is being done to death not in righteous fight but through wile. Since that could happen, he claims, only because he was away, he has now the natural obligation of avenging Duryodhana. The very next moment, however, a change appears to come over him. Instead of arrogantly piling up hyperboles as before, he lowers his voice for a moment, and reflects how even warriors greater than him had been trounced by the Pandavas[23] (Verse 58). But before this mood can gain ascendency in his mind he looks intently at Duryodhana lying sprawled out on the ground. The native lustre and majesty of Duryodhana's personality is feelingly captured[24] in one of the verses he then recites (verse 59). The pathetic scene induces a fresh wave of indignation in his mind, and so great is its intensity that he can only exclaim in a voice quivering with suppressed passion, 'O king of Kurus, how is this!'.

Duryodhana realises at once that a crucial moment had arrived. He knows the temper of Aswattama well enough. In the past the sight of his preceptor's valiant son used to inspire in him a different set of emotions. But Aswatthama's tone and presence now fill him with uneasiness. In a calculated manner, therefore, he replies in a studied, calm tone of self–disparagement: 'This is the fruit of greed (ambition)'. He is unhesitatingly taking upon himself all the blame for his present state, and deliberately putting it in the form of an incontrovertible, self–explanatory, pithy judgment. He hopes thereby to mollify his irascible young general. This statement, once again revealing Duryodhana's new sense of humility and clear-sighted objectivity, deserves to be carefully noted.

Aswatthama refuses to lay down arms. Drawing a colourful picture of the Pandava–warriors in the company of Lord Krishna, he vows he would destroy them all even as they stood panoplied in full armour. He would tear them into pieces, 'as one might a canvas cluttered with the picture of well-armed warriors[25] (verse 60)'. The pluck and brazenness of Aswatthama could not have been better communicated than through this statement that the combined might of Krishna and the Pandavas is nothing more than a 'painted' power to him. One remembers the elaborate simile of the 'picture', used in the *Viskambhaka*, to describe the colourful landscape of Kurukshetra peopled with vast legions assembled from all over the country, with their dazzling armour and accoutrement. The *dhvani* (evocation) of '*samkirna citra lakshyamiva*' here is richly dramatic, indeed. The colourful, vast concourse of people, it indicates, has now shrunk to this small, battered group of personalities. The first half of Aswatthama's verse projects the concentrated might of the Pandavas in company with Sri Krishna – an imposing picture. The next line of his verse vauntingly converts it into an insubstantial show that held no terror for him. Aswatthama's bumptiousness and disdain are conveyed with neat precision.

Duryodhana counsels Aswatthama to give up his belligerent mood. In a voice of calm resignation and a mellow sense of disillusionment, Duryodhana appeals to him to rise above bellicose feelings and see the reality – all the great kings and warriors had already perished, and their leader himself was about to die. Aswatthama, for his part, tries to rouse Duryodhana into fury by bitterly reminding him that Bhima had ignominiously pulled him by the hair, and had smashed into pulp not only his thighs, but his reputation and honour, as well. This is an interesting moment, for, Duryodhana's moral and emotional state is being put to a searching test. Aswatthama seeks to rub him at his most vulnerable point – his royal pride and honour. In his reply, however, Duryodhana shows an extraordinary imperturbability. First of all, he counters Aswatthama in calm, deprecatory tone by saying his honour had not been affected and he was by no means compromising his majesty. After all, he now reminds Aswatthama, it was because of that proud, royal intransigence of his that he had cheerfully courted all the disaster. His reputation was safe, he repeats; but candidly adds, his evil conceit deserved to be shattered. Again, considering the kind of humiliations he had earlier meted out to the Pandavas, the unrighteous methods he had adopted and the torments he had devised for them, the recent action of Bhima, he affirms, can by no means be considered an outrageous piece of treachery.

The present sequence serves an important dramatic function. It is not designed simply as a repetition of the earlier pattern that was observed with Valarama displaying an indignant posture and

Duryodhana pleading with him to desist from reprisal action against Bhima – not another variation merely in the dramatization of provocation and incitement countered by moral firmness. One fundamental difference inheres in the fact that while Valarama is Duryodhana's preceptor, Aswatthama is only one of his leading warriors. A second point of difference relates to the present psychological state of Duryodhana who has just emerged from a deeply moving experience of personal mortification and grief. Since he knows Aswatthama is an invincible, ruthless fighter, one for whom no martial exploit could be considered altogether impossible, he should ordinarily have felt tempted to order immediate vengeance. The barbed words of Aswatthama, again, were particularly calculated to lash him into fury. In the face of all this, however, Duryodhana maintains his poise and persists in upholding higher values as before. His inner triumph, therefore, can no more be in doubt.

The unmistakeable moral and spiritual conviction of the protagonist supports the claim that what the play seeks to dramatize is moral victory and not tragic defeat. A profounder kind of hope and elation, different from a broad philosophical tone informing the mood of dejected surrender and disillusioned acceptance, as in Macbeth or Hamlet, controls the mood of the protagonist and lends to the play a special dignity. The so-called 'tragic' materials are, in fact, organised as a support, a reinforcement of its dominant mood of exaltation and glory. And that is one reason why it would be wrong to treat the play as similar to a Greek tragedy[26]. Admiration here is not meant to intensify pity; rather, the sequences of sorrow and 'pity' are organised as instruments for heightening admiration.

As has already been seen, a number of tragic features and intensely pathetic scenes are introduced. But they only serve as a stage, a process, in the greater amplification of the centrally developed note of moral and emotional exaltation. That is why, when Duryodhana dies on the stage (in clear violation of the injunction of Sanskrit canonists) at the end of the play, he is not only shown nursing a higher aspiration, but actually experiencing the magnificent consummation he had been hoping for. In his dying speech he declares that he is already seeing the spirits of his eminent ancestors and divine damsels waiting at the portals of heaven to welcome him. He announces in a jubilant voice the arrival of a heavenly car which has been sent by the Lord of Righteouness to fetch him. He also notes the presence of sacred rivers and oceans in their subtle essences, all waiting to sanctify his ascension. The supreme satisfaction and ecstasy experienced in his death, conveying as it does the basic feeling of the drama to a logical consummation negates all arguments about the play being a tragedy. Death here has no trace of the elements of horror, pity, or waste – possibly that is the reason why Bhasa, in spite of the warning of the canonists, did not shrink from portraying it on the stage.

The play, therefore, can be viewed as constituting a fundamental reversal of the tragic plot. It is, however, necessary to look into one of the last utterances of Duryodhana before finally coming to a conclusion on the ultimate mental state of the protagonist. The words in question introduce a note of contentment, which is entirely different in character form the one based on his ecstatic vision already alluded to. Just as Duryodhana is breathing his last, Aswatthama, on the strength of his ecclesiastical authority (*vipro-kteir Vachane*), declares that he is installing Durjaya as the king of Kurus, thus refusing to revise his pledge and to abide by Duryodhana's pasifirt counsel. He can fight the Pandavas only as a general of the Kuru king; and so crowns Durjaya king of the Kaurava lands–'both inherited and acquired' – signifying, by 'acquired', the Pandava territories over which the great war had been fought.[27] Immediately after, Duryodhana is heard expressing his satisfaction on this act of Aswatthama's. 'Ah, my heart's desire is fulfilled' (*'Hanta, krtam me hrdayanujan tam'*) he exclaims, and joyously goes forward to meet his death.

Crowning of Durjaya contains clear implications of perpetuation of hostilities. It implies passing on to Durjaya a burden of clan – warfare and bloody vendetta which Duryodhana had so thoughtfully avoided in his parting speech to the young prince. Duryodhana had not only expressly forbidden the others to take up arms on his behalf, he had also taken particular care to keep the mind of Durjaya untainted by any trace of antagonism against the Pandavas. On the other hand, the token ritual performed by Aswatthama has nothing ambiguous about it. Only a few moments before Valarama had ominously declared – in a voice expressing both anxiety and satisfaction–that Aswatthama was certain to mount a raid on the Pandava camp to kill off the Pandavas the same night. How, then, does Duryodhana express his 'satisfaction' over the crowning of Durjaya? Does it cancel out the earlier pacifist emphasis and revive the mood of belligerence just on the eve of his death ? If so, the question of his moral transformation would need to be re-examined. This could have far-reaching implications on the nature of the play as a whole. Moreover, it would stand as a fundamentally antithetical impulse in the context of his dying speech.

One might further note how, following the delineation of Duryodhana's death, the drama closes with the other major characters leaving the stage after they have expressed their individual future resolves. Aswatthama, who enjoys the emotional support of Valarama, declares his intransigent belligerency in unequivocal terms, emphasizing thereby a political, militant orientation of the close. Dhrutarastra, on the other hand, who departs from the stage in the other direction, announces his decision to renounce his kingdom and pursue the true wealth of life through penance and prayer, thus imparting to the conclusion a spiritual orientation. Durjaya, the innocent child whom both these announcements affect the most, stands in the middle, silent and uncomprehending. Does Bhasa, then, wish to leave the play emotionally (and morally) inconclusive at its end, pulled equally powerfully in the opposed directions of earthly passion and religious transcendence? In that case, the two contrary moods and tones apparently present in Duryodhana's final speech could also be legitimately interpreted as a deliberately organised ambivalence.

In fact, the entire play can be viewed from a certain perspective to show its progress all along through such ambivalence and emotional conflict. Natural human volitions pitted against a superior moral code, earthly passion and their transcendence, pathetic sentimentality and heroic calm – such contrasted elements have been emphasized and amplified through the introductory choric descriptions, as also various sequences and characters. Apparently a case can be made out to show that Bhasa is uneasily poised between two different orders of reality and two kinds of values. Equally plausibly it can be argued that he has deliberately kept the play free of simplistic resolution and has chosen, instead, to dramatise the tension of values in an eclectic manner.

Suppositions such as these would be difficult to admit, however, because of three factors. First of all, the nature and tradition of this drama commit it to the evocation of definite *rasas*. Secondly, the related cultural tradition (through which alone the meaning of the drama can be determined) had a positive, preponderant moral bias. Unlike Western drama where the central interest inheres in the 'humanistic' portrayal of conflict between the personal and the social, the mundane and the spiritual, Classical Sanskrit drama – particularly before and up to Kalidasa – operated within the ambit of a philosophical-intellectual scheme which comprehensively resolved all the diversities of life into a harmonious order. For instance, even violence and killing could be so chastened and elevated (partly as here in this play, or, more fully as in Bhagavad Gita) that, far from being sinful acts they could even confer religious merit. The mundane and the spiritual were not viewed as largely exclusive, opposed worlds, as in Christianity. Conflict, ambivalence or paradox issuing out of the tension between Christian (or Gnostic) and humanistic attitude which are often to be found at the core of most European dramas are rather out of place in the play world of Bhasa. Finally, the treatment of the protagonist, which is entirely oriented towards moral regeneration, would show that the dramatist cannot be seeking to incorporate some 'human' ambivalence into his final words.

As has been seen, Bhasa has radically transformed the original version of Vyasa where a mortally wounded Duryodhana gets Aswatthama ritually appointed commander in chief and solicits vendetta against the Pandavas. Vyasa nowhere portrays moral heightening of Duryodhana whose primary excellence is that of a valiant warrior, something that earns him even heavenly approbation. It is unthinkable that having recreated the character the way he has, Bhasa would introduce an element to negate at the end the entire rendering. In reality, Duyodhana's expression of satisfaction on the token consecration of Durjaya is nothing more than an immediate, natural, filial response. With this he is shown withdrawing into himself and passing away, focussing on spiritual prospects ahead. Durjaya's symbolic crowning, in itself, would not be a categorical instruction for, or endorsement of, further hostilities.

Duryodhana's attitude to the act of provisional crowning being fundamentally different from Aswtthama's, there can be no justification for grafting on an innocent impulsive expression of his such belligerent intentions as are obvious in the latter. Similarly, it would be incorrect to read any tonal – that is to say, moral – uncertainty in the delineation of the contrasted aspirations of Dhrutarastra and Aswatthama at the conclusion of the play. After the main event, that is, after Duryodhana's moral regeneration is fully portrayed, the playwright merely indicates in passing, how general life continues to remain what it always was – a mixture of peace and violence, sadness and elation, detachment and worldliness. Between the extreme moods of cynical revulsion against life, and passionate involvement in its verities – between the two contrasted affirmations by Dhrutarastra and Aswatthama – Duryodhana's moral elevation is set off all the more luminously.

Although the two characters in question project two contrasted attitudes to war, they are not organised as culminating dramatic images. The main business of the drama being already over, these subsidiary characters are only being provided a convenient exit. Their words are meant to suitably round off the dramatic action – nothing more. Since the audience was familiar with the later developments as they occur in the *Mahabharata* and since the play was about Duryodhana there could be no intention on the part of the playwright to highlight at the conclusion the disaster to come. Fittingly enough is sounded a note of aesthetic objectivity – also a feeling of wholesomeness – through the *Bharatavakya*, imparting a mood of happy quietude.

Urubhangam, therefore, constitutes an illustrative modification of the tragic mode. It incorporates diverse kinds of material that are productive of an intensely tragic mood, but manipulates them into heartening experiences. Neither in the style of a conventional tragi-comedy, nor in the spirit of the passion – play, does it provide tragic episodes merely to oppose and negate them at the end with some joyous development. It propels one inexorably through a vast stretch of tragic anguish to a climax of death and desolation, but transforms the entire proceeding by organising a pervasive tone of moral exaltation, and converting the moment of death into one of profound triumph. It is as if Bhasa had set himself the task of not just rejecting, but metamorphosing, the tragic muse.

Notes and References

1. The manner in which the status of a Tragedy is appropriated for the play by Kapildev Giri, at the same time as its traditional features in line with *Natya Sastra* are emphasized, is illustrative. See, Kapildev Giri (ed.), *Urubhangam*, Chowkhamba Vidyabhavan, Varanasi, 1968, p. 17. It is interesting to note that, to the majority of commentators on Sanskrit drama, the delineation of Duryodhana's death has been the most – almost the only – remarkable feature of the play. This, for instance, is the only point Dr. Suryakant finds worth mentioning about *Urubhangam* in a general survey of Sanskrit drama. See, Nagendra (ed.), *Bharatiya Natya Sahitya*, S. Chand and Co., 1968......
2. A.B.Keith, *The Sanskrit Drama*, Oxford University Publication, 1970 Reprint – pp. 277-280.
3. Ibid.: "Duryodhana is the chief subject but not the hero of the piece" (p. 106). And, ".... it is a mere reading of modern sentiment into ancient literature to treat Duryodhana in the *Urubhangam* as the hero of the drama" (p. 278).

4. One of the recent historical studies, *Indian Kavya Literature*, Vol. II, (A.K.Warder, Motilal Banarasidass, Delhi, 1974, p. 950) discusses *Urubhangam* as a tragedy–as if it were an established critical view.

5. "Bharata's *Natya Sastra* which came to be strictly enforced, at any rate, since the time of Kalidasa, accounts for the absence of tragedy in later dramas." A.D.Pusalker, *Bhasa: A Study*, Munshiram Manoharlal, Delhi, Second Edition, 1968, p. 140.

6. H.W.Wells calls it a tragic play; in reality, it is a heroic play with its focus on the magnificent resolution, and on the valour of its protagonist in the face of a totally desperate situation. The play concludes with Karna moving forward to give battle in an entirely defenceless condition, but with an optimistic frame of mind. This clearly indicates the emphasis of the play. The later events to which this situation leads in the original epic may, or may not, be tragic. But to take *Karnabharam* as a play designed to conclude with a desolate, tragic perspective, is to completely misread it.

7. For instance, Kailashpati Ojha, *Hindi Trasadi: Siddhanta Aur Parampara*, Sahitya Sadan, Dehra Dun, 1968, Ch. III, pp. 114-164.

8. Critics like Dr. S.K.De do not seem to have properly explained the dramatic significance of the *Viskambhaka* in *Urubhangam.* See, S.N.Dasgupta and S.K.De, *History of Sanskrit Literature*, University of Calcutta, 1977,p. 113.

9. Dramatic appropriateness of every small element in Bhasa's plays may be observed here from the apparently non-significant introduction of a male attendant, instead of the conventional stage-manager's wife, while laying the *Sthapana.* The matter at hand being heroic, as also horrifying, the playwright has deliberately chosen a male companion for the *Sutradhara.*

10. The huge mythical serpent which was tied as a rope round mount Mandara by gods and demons when they churned the ocean of milk.

11. *Urubhangam*, 31,33.

12. Ibid., 36.

13. Ibid., 40.

14. Ibid., 38.

15. Ibid., 43.

16. Bhola Shankar Vyas', *(Sanskrita Kavi Darshana*, The Chowkhamba vidyabhavan, Varanasi, 1968), stands out among famous works of criticism on Sanskrit literature for its total incomprehension of Bhasa's dramatic achievement:

Bhasa's plays – if they were originally as we see them today – are bereft of artistic beauty like the 'Miracles' and 'Moralities' which came before Shakespeare: they have neither a mature kind of dramatic organisation of subject-matter and psychological delineation of character: nor a grand poetic style.... (p. 250)

17. *Urubhangam*, 47.
18. Ibid.,, 49.
19. Ibid., 50.
20. Ibid., 53.
21. Ibid., 55.
22. Ibid., 57. and prose dialogues after it.
23. Ibid., 58.
24. Ibid., 59.
25. Ibid., 60.
26. R.N.Singhal (*Aristotle* and *Bharata*, 1977, p. 97) misses the quality of the organisation of tragic material in *Urubhangam*.

    This Sanskrit play, a solitary composition of its kind, comes very close to Greek Tragedy. The central idea of Greek Tragedy is that man learns through suffering, and it is through suffering that he becomes modest and humble. Man realises the futility of ambition and accepts his own insignificance. But before he learns his lesson, he has to pay heavily for it;... that is what happens in *Urubhangam*.
27. *Urubhangam*, 65.

Index